Jumping, Laughing & Resting

By Evelyn Challis.

Amsco Publications
New York/London/Sydney

Contents

Cover art direction by Mike Bell
Cover illustration by Graham Percy
Text illustrations by Melanie Gaines Arwin
Book design by Iris Weinstein

Copyright © 1974 by Oak Publications,
A Division of Embassy Music Corporation, New York
Published 1984 by Amsco Publications,
A Division of Music Sales Corporation, New York
All Rights Reserved

ISBN No:0.8256.0158.2
Library of Congress Catalog Card Number: 74-80282

Exclusive Distributors:
Music Sales Corporation
225 Park Avenue South, New York, NY 10003 USA
Music Sales Limited
8/9 Frith Street, London W1V 5TZ England
Music Sales Pty. Limited
120 Rothschild Street, Rosebery, Sydney NSW 2018 Australia

Printed in the United States of America by
Vicks Lithograph and Printing Corporation

Introduction

How can you decide which songs to teach children to sing? There are funny songs, work songs, love songs, and spirituals. You may like one song for its lovely or haunting melody while liking another for its refrain. Then of course there are the songs that tell gripping stories or communicate important messages with well-turned phrases.

A song can be any number of things. But most important of all it must be one that *you,* the person teaching it, loves as well as one that you think the children (with their special backgrounds, ages, and experiences) will also love.

In my experience with children I've discovered that the best method to "teach" a song was simply to sing it in its entirety and ask them to join in when they felt they knew it. Very seldom did I use the *rote* method of singing a line at a time, then going back to repeat it. Music for beginners can be so much fun and enjoyment. I think it can be too easily spoiled for children by making it hard work. In general my basic attitude in the classroom, at home, and in assemblies has been: "Here's a song, I think you'll love, let's see how well you like it." I would then sing the song. If I was correct about their loving it they'd ask for it again and again. Soon they would be singing it with me. Occasionally, I'd stop and go over one or two of the difficult phrases.

One thing more: *There's no such thing as a non-singer!* How many of you were forever cut off from singing during your childhood by a teacher who insisted that you mouth the words? Uh-uh! No more of that. Everybody can sing.

If you have ever watched kids sing songs they love—and love singing them, you will understand why I think it less important that they be sung perfectly; why I feel the attitude of enjoyment and love is far more important.

Understand that I am not talking about a trained chorus for which I used to audition kids by singing a harmony into their ear while they sang the melody of a familiar tune. If they stayed on the melody they were in, if not, they weren't. Above all, they didn't go away feeling they were non-singers! They felt encouraged that they would sing another day, that they might qualify for another chorus but would need more ear-training and practice. In the meantime there would always be the great songfests in Assemblies and Classrooms in which they could join in at the top of their voices!

So there you have the intent of this book: to provide the material together with a few simple instructions to help parents and teachers involve children in the joy of expressing themselves through song. Some were taught to me by children. Many we sang without accompaniment; most I accompanied with my guitar. Some of the Action Songs were sung with piano while I led the movements in front of the Assembly. Some songs I've simply sung to children or had a child sing solo in one of our concerts. In concerts I've presented (including one with 80 voices) I've accompanied most songs on my guitar.

The following code identifies the way a song may be used. Please use the code only as a guide and experiment with it in your own way.

A— Assembly
C— Classroom
S— Solo
SC— Selected Chorus
E— Ensemble (usually 6 to 12 voices).

I add my thanks to those who have been so helpful during those years when I was compiling this volume: Irwin Silber who provided me with the much needed encouragement to begin, Liz Scott, Alice Ostrowsky, Laura Ostrowsky, Anne Shure and Sue Pearlgut and Connie Laurie Lukiean who provided me with lost verses to scraps of melodies lurking in my head; Sy Goldman who spent many hours transcribing and copying words and music; and, of course, Pierre Gerard Nau, whose patient and gentle prodding kept me going. Special thanks to Pete Seeger and Malvina Reynolds, Ed Lipton and Joyce Ringdahl Susskind for their generosity in donating their songs to what they recognized as a labor of love. Additional thanks go to the anonymous children and adults whose singing (to me, for me and with me), writings and recordings make up the bulk of this volume.

Evelyn Challis

Index of Song Titles

Index of First Lines

Guitar Chords

This sign means that the two strings may be played simultaneously

x
This cross means that the string should not be sounded

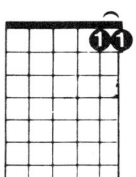 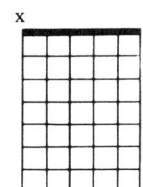

A    A⁷ 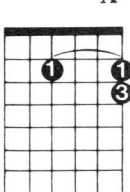   Am    Am⁷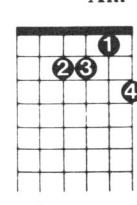

B 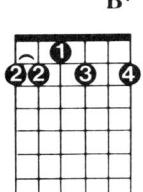   B⁷   Bm 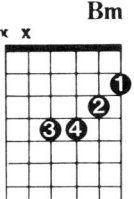   C 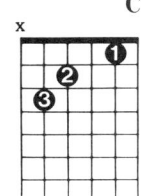   C⁷ 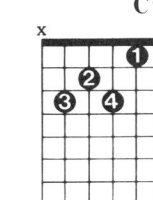   Cm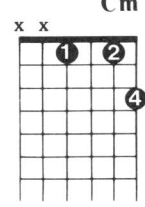

D 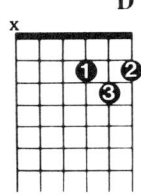   D⁷ 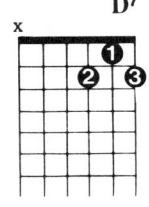   Dm 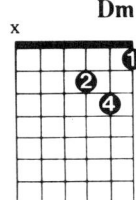   Dm⁷ 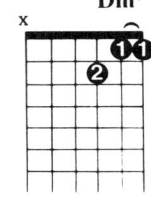   E 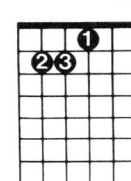   E⁷    Em    Em⁷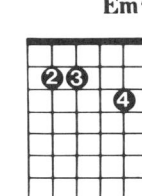

F 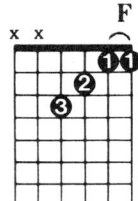   Fm 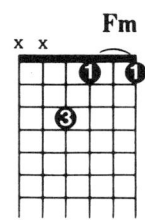   F♯ 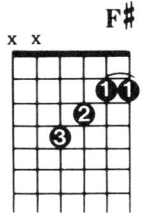   F♯m 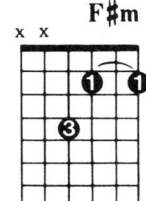   G 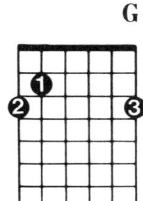   G⁷ 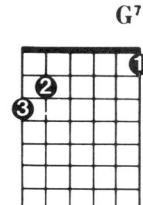   Gm 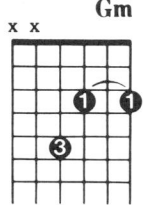   Gm⁷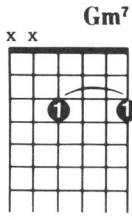

Major Keys

I	IV	V⁷
A	D	E⁷
B	E	F♯⁷
C	F	G⁷
D	G	A⁷
E	A	B⁷
F	B♭	C⁷
F♯	B	C♯⁷
G	C	D⁷

Minor Keys

I	IV	V⁷
Am	Dm	E⁷
Bm	Em	F♯⁷
Cm	Fm	G⁷
Dm	Gm	A⁷
Em	Am	B⁷
Fm	B♭m	C⁷
F♯m	Bm	C♯⁷
Gm	Cm	D⁷

Jumping, Laughing and Resting

Songs for Fingers, Thumbs, Hands and Feet.

"Ha! Ha! This A-Way!"

The songs here are among those little children love most. They're fun to teach and it's a delight to watch children imitating the leader's movements. Usually, in the classroom, since I was so busy with the movements of the song, I would teach them unaccompanied. However, in assemblies, most of the time there will be someone who can vamp the simple chords and melodies on the piano. Actually no accompaniment is necessary since these songs are quite complete in themselves. In one or two of them—such as *This Old Man*—an accompaniment would interfere with your slowing down or speeding up the rhythm according to your whim—which adds to the children's delight in trying to follow you. Sometimes you might find a pianist who would join in and follow you.

Of the following, all are action songs; the first three are also rounds. Of the last six singing games, three were taught to me by my Puerto Rican students.

Where Is Thumbkin?

North American
Tune: *Frére Jacques*

F
Where is Thumbkin? Where is Thumbkin?

Both hands behind back.

C⁷
Here I am, here I am.

One hand comes out with thumb up on each "Here I am."

F
How are you today, Sir?

Left thumb "asks" right thumb by bouncing up and down 4 times on the beat; right thumb answers in the same way.

Very well I thank you,

   C⁷ F
Run a-way,

Right hand goes behind back.

   C⁷ F
Run a-way.

Left hand goes behind back.

Where is Pointer? etc.

Index finger.

Where is Middle-man? etc.

Middle finger.

Where is Ring-man? etc.

Ring finger.

Where is Little-man? etc.

Little finger.

For classroom use this delightful action song is sung straight. But in assembly, I could never resist dividing the auditorium into 4 groups, trying it as a round. The result may look a little chaotic, but it usually *sounds* good and it's always great fun!

Why Doesn't My Goose?

English

C   G⁷   C   C   G⁷   C
Why doesn't my goose pay as much as thy goose,

C   G⁷   C   C   G⁷   C
When I paid for my goose twice as much as thine?

The only action in this song is to jump out of your seat when you get to the third *"goose,"* sitting down again quietly on the line *"twice as much as thine."* Try it first just straight. Then, in assembly, try it in 2 Parts. When you think they're good enough, try it in four parts and be prepared to laugh!

(A , C)

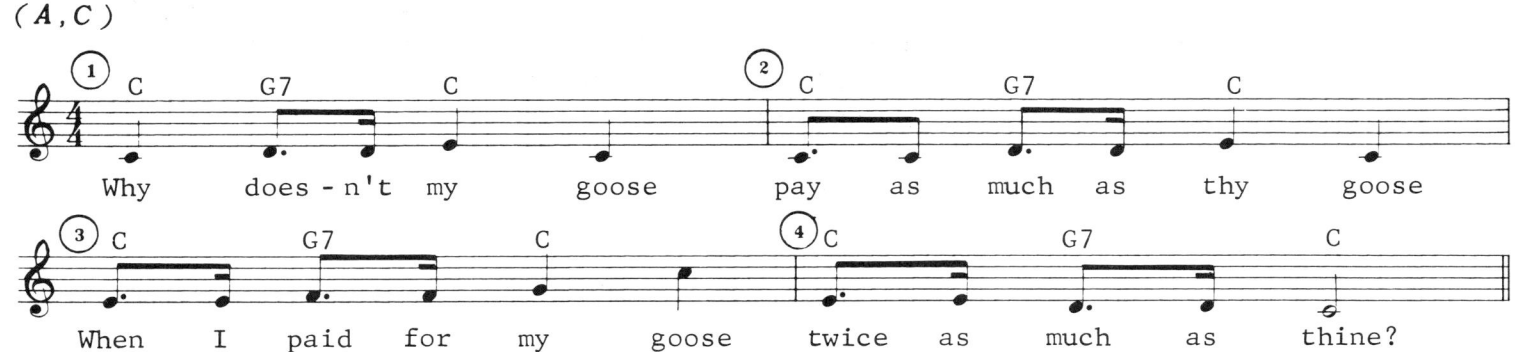

Little Tommy Tinker

English

C
Little Tom Tinker sat on a clinker,

And he began to cry:

"Ma! Ma!

          G⁷   C
Poor little innocent I!"

Again, the only action in this song is to jump out of your seat, throwing your arms up to the sky, mouth wide open, alarm written all over your face, and sit down again *quickly* on *each* "Ma!" When this song is divided into 4 parts the results are hilarious. So far, I have not been able to get all the way through it on the first try. On the second or third try it sounds pretty nice.

11

The Teensy-Weensy Spider

North American

D
Oh the teensy-weensy spider climbed

　G　　A⁷　　D
　up the water-spout.

Simulate a spider crawling up the spout by joining the index finger of one hand to the thumb of the other, then the thumb of one hand to the index finger of the other, etc.

Down came the rain and

　G　　　　A⁷　　D
　washed the spider out!

Motion the rain coming down and sweeping the spider out.

Out came the sun and

　G　　A⁷　　D
　dried up all the rain,

Show the sun coming out with both arms forming an arc above head; show the drying up of all the rain by warm rays coming down—moving fingers as if playing the piano.

And the teensy-weensy spider climbed

　G　　A⁷　　D
　up the spout again!

Repeat the original "climbing" action.

Six Little Ducks

North American

D A⁷ Six little ducks that I once knew,	Hold up 6 fingers.
D Fat ones, skinny ones, there were two;	Show "fat" and "skinny" with hands, hold up 2 fingers on "two."
A⁷ But the one with the feathers upon his back:	Hands behind back, fingers fluttering.

D   A⁷   D

He ruled the others with his "Quack, quack, quack!   Tuck hands in armpits, move elbows up and down 3 times, once on each quack.

Chorus:

                        A⁷   D

Quack, quack, quack. Quack, quack, quack!"   Repeat last action 6 times, once on each quack.

                       A⁷   D

He ruled the others with his "Quack, quack, quack!"   Repeat last action 3 times, once on each quack.

Down the river they would go, etc.   Point down.

Wibble, wabble, wibble, wabble, to and fro,   Imitate ducks *wibble-wabbling* by putting both palms together, and moving them back and forth
    etc.

Home from the river they would come, etc.   Motion "Come here" with arm.

Wibble, wabble, wibble, wabble, ho-hum-hum!,   Imitate ducks again.
    etc.   Yawn and mock sleep with both hands at side of head.

This Old Man

Irish

C
This old man, he played one,   Hold up one finger.

F   G⁷
He played nick-nack on my thumb,   Tap thumb-nails together.

          C
With a nick-nack paddy-whack give a dog a bone,   Keep tapping thumb-nails.

G   G⁷   C
This old man came rolling home.   Fold arms, make rolling motion with fore-arms
                                                       going in circle; end with hands behind back.

This old man, he played two...shoe, etc.   Same except tap shoe.

This old man, he played three...knee, etc.   Same except tap knee.

Four...floor, etc.   Same except tap floor.

Five...hive, etc.   Tap both sides of head with both hands.

Six...sticks, etc.   Tap index fingers together.

Seven...up in heaven, etc.   Point thumbs skyward in time to the music.

Eight...at my gate, etc.   Tap forehead.

Nine...on my spine, etc.   Run thumb up and down spine.

Ten...once again, etc.   Open and close both hands showing all ten
                                                       fingers on open hands, in time to music.

The children get a big kick out of trying to follow you if you vary the speed of the song, especially on the last line "This old man came rolling home." Sometimes I draw this out and throw in a few yawns and other times I zip through it so fast that my hands are behind my back while they're still "rolling!"

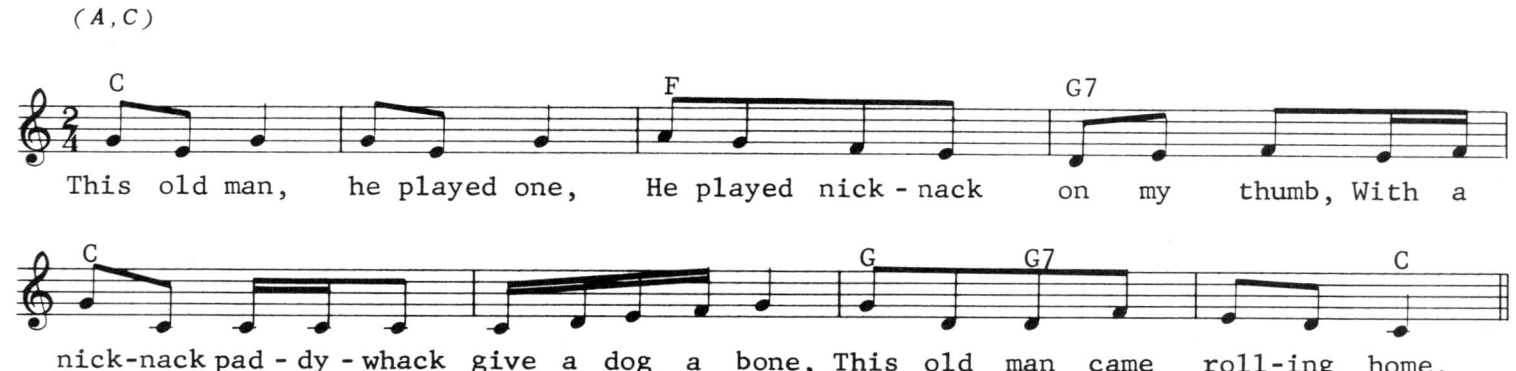

14

One Finger, One Thumb, One Hand

North American

C
One finger, one thumb, one hand keep moving,

One finger, one thumb, one hand keep moving,

One finger, one thumb, one hand keep moving,

    G⁷   C
And we'll all be happy and gay.

One finger, one thumb, one hand,
   two hands keep moving, etc.
One finger, one thumb, one hand,
   two hands, one foot keep moving, etc.
One finger, one thumb, one hand,
   two hands, one foot, two feet
   keep moving, etc.
One finger, one thumb, one hand,
   two hands, one foot, two feet,
   get up, turn around,
   sit down keep moving, etc.

Index finger, then your thumb, then your whole hand up & down in time to the music.

At the right moment add 2nd hand.

At the right moment add tapping foot.

Add 2 tapping or stomping feet.

Just follow what it says.

Don't worry about the timing of this song. As each appendage is added you take all kinds of liberty with the timing. The important thing here is the *action!*

Ha-Ha This A-Way!

Huddie Ledbetter
Collected and adapted by John A. and Alan Lomax

D   A⁷ D
When I was a little boy, little boy, little boy,
        A⁷   D
When I was a little boy, twelve years old,
       A⁷ D
Papa went and left me, left me, left me,
       A⁷   D
Papa went and left me, bless my soul!

Chorus: (2x)
D   G A⁷
Ha! Ha! this-a-way, Ha! Ha! that-a-way,

D   G A⁷ D
Ha! Ha! this-a-way, Then, oh, then!

Mama come and got me, got me, got me,
Mama come and got me, to save my soul,
Mama didn't whip me, whip me, whip me,
Mama didn't whip me, so I's told.

I went to school, etc.
Teacher didn't whip me, etc.

Learned my lesson, etc.
Wasn't that a blessin'? etc.

Liked my teacher, etc.
Prayed like a preacher, etc.

The action in this song is with the chorus. The leader makes any movement that can be thought up in time to the music. While singing each verse the leader can pick someone who will lead the action when the chorus comes around again.

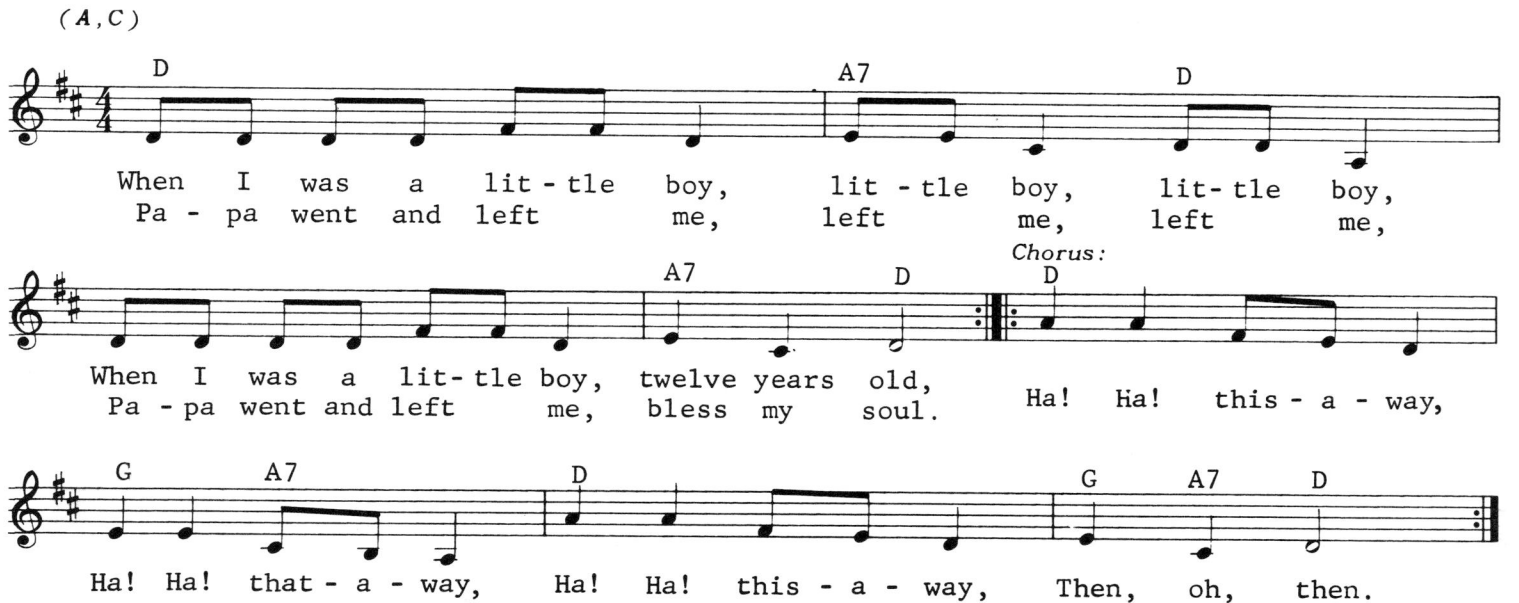

I'm A Little Teapot

English

A   D   A
I'm a little teapot short and stout,

D   A   E⁷   A
Here is my handle, here is my spout,

                  D A
When I get all steamed up, then I shout:

   D   E⁷   A
"Just tip me over and pour me out!"

Make appropriate actions to describe shortness and fatness.

Left hand on hip—handle; right hand forms spout—right elbow on hip.

Hold the above pose through this line.

Tip body from waist to the right in the direction of spout and you are pouring the tea out!

The Wheels On The Bus

North American

E
The wheels on the bus go 'round and 'round,

B⁷   E
'Round and 'round, 'Round and 'round,

The wheels on the bus go 'round & 'round,

B⁷   E
All through the town.

The money in the box goes
    "Clink! Clink! Clink! etc.

The wipers on the bus go
    "Swish! Swish! Swish! etc.

The driver on the bus goes
    "Move on back!" etc.

The people on the bus go
    up and down, etc.

Fold arms, make a rolling motion by going in circles in time to the music. For variety, change the direction of the roll away from you to toward you. Also change the speed of the song.

Put two hands together as if you have a lot of change in them and shake hands in time to music.

Make your forearms be the wipers, attached to the windshield by the elbows—wipe back and forth in time to the music.

Use your best thumbing hitch-hiker pose for this verse.

Bend your knees, unbend them, bend them, etc. In this way you can go up and down all through this verse.

18

Jim Along Josie

English

D
Hi! .... Slap knees twice.

Ho! .... Clap hands twice.

Jim along .... Snap fingers of both hands
to your right side.

Josie, ... Snap fingers of both hands
to your left side.

Hi! .... Raise right shoulder.

Ho! .... Raise left shoulder.

A⁷
Jim along .... Lower first right and then left shoulder.

D
Jo! .... Drop head, chin on chest.
(On repeat, stamp feet twice as well as
dropping head, chin on chest.)

The main idea to this song is that you repeat it as often as you wish and each time you repeat it you get faster. It ends with almost a collapse!

In A Cabin In The Woods

English

C   F   G⁷
In a cabin in the woods,

          C
Little man by the window stood,

          G⁷
Little rabbit hopping by,

         C
Knocking at my door.

"Help me, help me, help!" he said,

  G⁷   C
" 'Fore the hunter shoot me dead!"

               G⁷
"Little rabbit come inside,

         C
Safely you'll abide."

Form a roof over your head with your hands.

Put one hand to eyes as a hunter would to see far.

Use two fingers in a "V" and hop along in time—4 hops.

Knock at imaginary door in time to music—5 knocks.

Start with fists at temples and on each "Help!" move both arms straight up into the air and put on a face of great alarm.
Form a gun with your hand and point at someone in the audience.

Motion for rabbit to come in with one hand—4 motions.

Hold imaginary rabbit in one arm and stroke it with the other—3 strokes.

This song becomes progressively shorter each time you sing it. Sing it through as is the first time. The second time, when you get to the line *"safely you'll abide"* make only the motion of stroking the rabbit 3 times but you sing nothing. On this line show the children that your lips are tightly closed. The third time do not sing on the last two lines *"Little rabbit come inside, safely you'll abide"* and you are left with just the motions. Only the motions are repeated each time you do a verse until on the 9th verse you are left with *only* the motions and no song! That is why this song is such fun.

20

My Hat It Has Three Corners

Italian

F   G⁷

F G^7
My hat it has three corners,

                       C
Three corners has my hat,

      G^7
And had it not three corners,

               C
It would not be my hat.

1st Time   Sing it through once just the way it is.

2nd Time   On "hat" don't sing anything but instead touch top of head.

3rd Time   Keep the action for "hat" and add to it holding up three fingers every time you come to the word "three."

4th Time   Keep the actions for "hat" and "three" and add to it holding up an elbow every time you come to the word "corners." Remember that whenever you have an action you do not sing that word.

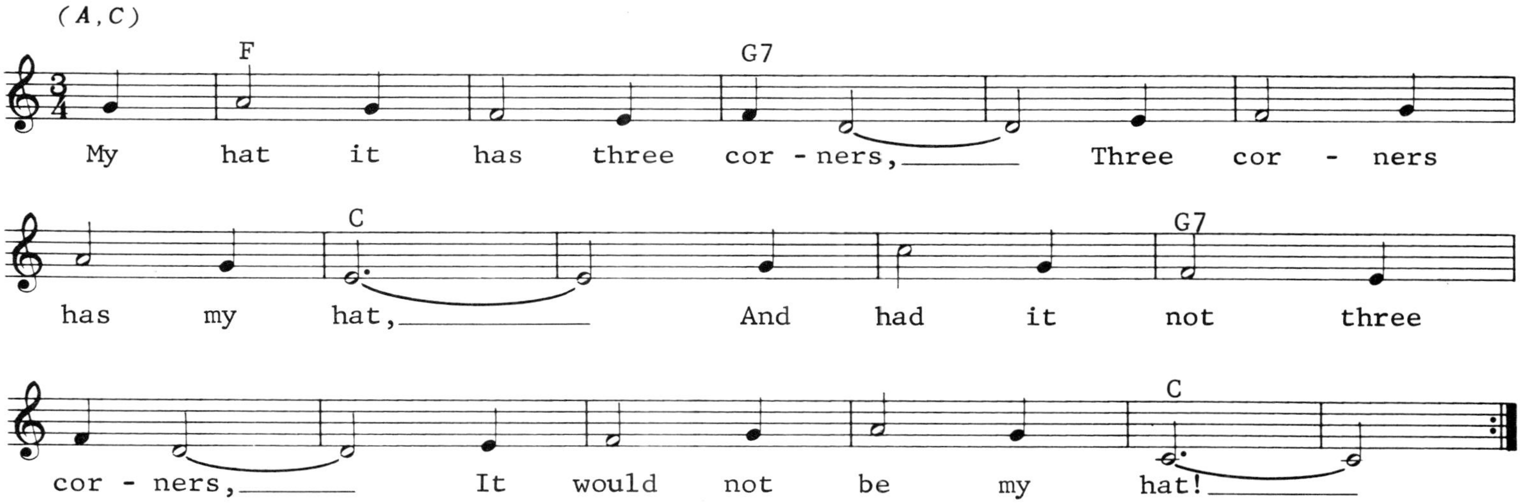

21

Bingo!

North American

```
        E          A    E        B⁷   E
There was a farmer had a dog and Bingo was his name, Sir!

    A    B⁷ E      A
B-I-N-G-O! B-I-N-G-O! B-I-N-G-O!

    B⁷          E
And Bingo was his name, Sir!
```

1st Time   Sing it through once just the way it is, hands behind back.

2nd Time   On every **B** when spelling it out don't sing, clap once instead.

3rd Time   On every **B** and **I** don't sing, clap twice instead.

4th Time   Clap on every **B I** and **N**.

5th Time   Clap on every **B I N** and **G**.

6th Time   Clap on every **B I N G** and **O**.

7th Time   Turn sideways and "clap" by missing your hands thereby creating total silence.

Remember to keep your hands behind your back whenever you're not using them!

22

Underneath The Spreading Chestnut Tree

English

```
C                           G⁷  C
Underneath the spreading chestnut tree,

      F          C
I'm as happy as can be;

F         G⁷     C
With my banjo on my knee,

                        G⁷  C
Underneath the spreading chestnut tree.
```

1st Time   Sing it through once just as it is with hands behind back.

2nd Time   On "spreading" instead of singing, make a spreading motion with your hands (hands together and then move them apart).

3rd Time   Keep the motion for "spreading" and add hitting yourself on the chest with your fist every time you come to the word "chest."

4th Time   Keep the motions for "spreading" and "chest" clunking yourself on the head every time you come to the word "nut."

5th Time   Keep the motions for "spreading" "chest" and "nut"; add putting both hands up about head-high, imitating a tree every time you come to the word "tree."

6th Time   Keep the motions for "spreading" "chest" "nut" and "tree" and add a big silent smile and point to your mouth when you come to the word "happy."

7th Time   Keep the motions for "spreading" "chest" "nut" "tree" and "happy" and add an imitation of a banjo player (clutch an imaginary banjo and strum down twice) when you come to the word "banjo."

Don't forget to keep your hands behind your back whenever you're not using them!

The Wild Oak Tree

North American

Verse:

Chord	Lyric	Action description	Action
C	Love grows	Slap knees twice.	Action A
	under the	Clap hands twice.	Action B
F	wild oak	Snap fingers of both hands to your right side.	Action C
C	tree,	Snap fingers of both hands to your left side.	Action D
F	Sugar	Wiggle both hands in front of you, right above left.	Action E
C	melts like	Wiggle both hands in front of you, left above right.	Action F
G^7	can-	Snap fingers of both hands over your right shoulder.	Action G
	dy;	Snap fingers of both hands over your left shoulder.	Action H
F	Top of the		Action A
G^7	mountain		Action B
F	shines like		Action C
C	gold and you		Action D
	kiss yer little		Action E
G^7	feller sorta		Action F
C	han-		Action G
	dy.		Action H

Refrain:

F
Dreams,   Action A

dreams,   Action B

C
sweet   Action C

dreams,   Action D

F
under the   Action E

G^7
wild oak   Action F

C
tree-e-e-e,   Action G

e-e-e-e-.   Action H

F
Dreams,   Action A

dreams,   Action B

C
sweet   Action C

dreams,   Action D

D
One for   Action E

you and   Action F

G^7
me!   Action G

So!   Action H

Back to the beginning; end on "Handy."

(A,C)

Verse:

Love grows un-der the wild oak tree, Su-gar melts like can-dy; Top of the moun-tain shines like gold and you kiss yer lit-tle fel-ler sort-a hand-y. Dreams, dreams, sweet dreams, un-der the wild oak tree-e-e-e. Dreams, dreams, sweet dreams, One for you and me, So!

The Noble Duke Of York

English

```
        G                    D⁷
Oh the noble Duke of York, he had ten thousand men,

  G            C              G     D⁷   G
He always led them up the hill, and he led them down again!

                                       D⁷
And when they were up they were up, and when they were down they were down,

  G                    C                 G     D⁷   G
And when they were neither up nor down, they were neither up nor down!
```

There are only two actions in this song: every time you come to the word "up", everybody stands, and every time you come to the word "down," everyone sits down. The last line is quite active.

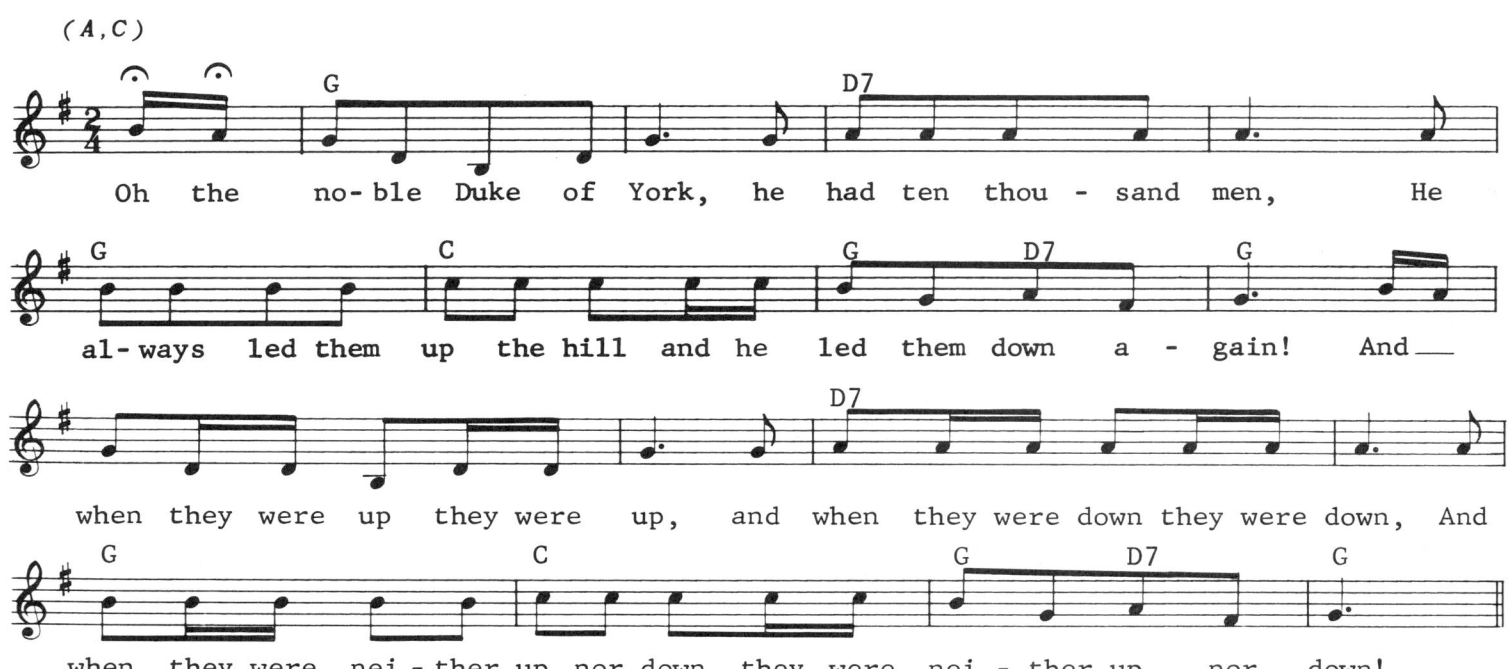

I Don't Want To March In The Infantry

North American

D
I don't want to march in the infantry,

A⁷
Shoot in the artillery,

D
Ride in the cavalry,

I don't want to fly over Germany,

A⁷   D
I just wanna be friends, *"Hi!"*

Refrain:

D   G   D
I just wanna be friends, *"Hi!"*

     A⁷   D
I just wanna be friends, *"Hi!"*

Back to beginning: end on first *"Hi!"*

March in place 4 steps on "march in the infantry".

Both hands "shoot" 4 times.

Hold "reins" and bend and straighten knee twice.

Flap arms 4 times on "fly".

Wave at someone on "Hi!".

Wave again.

And again.

27

Wasn't That A Band?

Afro-American

```
        E                                    B⁷
There was one, there were two, there were three little angels,

        E                                    B⁷
There were four, there were five, there were six little angels,

        E                                    B⁷
There were seven, there were eight, there were nine little angels,

E       B⁷   E
Ten little angels in that band!
```

Chorus:

```
   E
Oh, wasn't that a band? Sunday mornin'!

B⁷             E
Sunday mornin'! Sunday mornin'!
```

Wasn't that a band? Sunday mornin'!

```
A      B⁷   E
Sunday mornin' tune!
```

A song for as many rhythm instruments as you can find: drums, cymbals, triangles, rhythm sticks and anything else that can be hit or shook to make a sound or (let's face it) a noise! Give all instruments out with the explicit instruction that anyone playing their instrument *before* you say "Ready!" will forfeit their turn. Give 10 children a number from 1-10. Everyone sings the verse and each child hits his instrument once when his number comes up. Then, on the chorus, everybody joins in and plays their instrument in time to the music. It'll be loud but fun!

(A,C)

(A, C)

E .... B7 ... E .... *Chorus:* ... E

Ten lit -tle an -gels in that band!_____ Oh! was -n't that a

E B7

band?_____ Sun - day morn - in'! Sun - day morn - in'!

E

Sun - day morn - in'! Was -n't that a band?_____ Sun - day

B7 .... E

morn - in'! Sun - day morn - in' tune!_____

The Muffin Man

North American

E   F♯   B⁷
Oh, do you know the muffin man, the muffin man, the muffin man?

E   F♯   B⁷   E
Oh, do you know the muffin man who lives across the way?

Oh, yes I know the muffin man, the muffin man, the muffin man,
Oh, yes I know the muffin man who lives across the way.

One child is blindfolded while the others form a circle around him. They all sing the first verse. Only one child from the circle sings the second verse. If the child in the center can guess who is singing, he sings his own third verse: "Henry saw the muffin man"... etc., and then Henry is blindfolded and the game continues.

Paw Paw Patch

Traditional

D
Where, oh where, is dear little *(child's name)*?

A7   A
Where, oh where, is dear little Nellie?

D
Where, oh where, is dear little Nellie?

A⁷   D
'Way down yonder in the paw paw patch.

Come on boys, let's go find her, etc.

Pickin' up paw paws, puttin' 'em in your pocket, etc.

The children line up by couples, girls on the boys' right. On Verse 1, the first girl in line walks around both the boys' and her own line and back into place. (Use her name in singing.) On Verse 2, she does the same thing but this time all the boys follow her. On Verse 3, they ''peel off'': the boys following in a line as the first boy turns sharply to his left and the girls following in a line as the first girl turns sharply to her right. When the first couple meet they form an arch under which all the others pass. As they are singing this verse they are also acting out, picking up paw paws and putting them in a basket. Now there is a new first couple and the game continues. It may also be played by looking for a boy.

Francisco

Puerto Rican

D
Take off your shoes and stockings,

A⁷
And if your feet go bare,

Fran-C-I-S-CO, C-I-S-CO,

D
Shake it if you care, Oh!

Shake it baby, shake it,
Shake it if you care,
Fran-C-I-S-CO, C-I-S-CO,
Shake it if you care, Oh!

Tumble to the bottom,
Tumble to the top,
Turn yourself around and 'round,
And then you STOP!

''Francisco'' is standing still in the middle of the circle while all the others are moving around him with their hands joined and are singing the song to him.

''Francisco'' puts his hands on hips and by bending first one knee and then the other, he manages to ''shake it.'' The others are standing still and clapping in time to the music.

''Francisco'' and the others stoop and point to the floor, then they stand on tiptoe and point as high as they can. While ''Francisco'' turns himself around and 'round with his eyes closed and pointed finger outstretched, the others stand still and wait for him to come to ''STOP!'' Whoever he is pointing to is the next ''Francisco''or ''Francisca''.

Arroz Con Leche (Rice with Milk)

Chilean

Chorus:

```
E                         B⁷   A    E    B⁷   E
```
Arroz con leche se quiere casar con una viudita de la capital,

```
                          B⁷                        E
```
Que sepa tejer, que sepa bordar, y ponga la aguja en su telar.

Soy una viuda, mi padre, un rey; quiero casarme y no encuentro con quién,
Con tú, tal vez, con tú, no, no; con tú, sí, sí, sí, al iglesia vámos.

Translation:

White rice tastes delicious with sugar and milk, who'll marry a widow with hair just like silk,
Who knows how to sew, who knows how to cook; who washes, and irons, and reads from a book?
I am a widow, my father's the king; I want to get married and wear a fine ring,
With you, I might; with you, Oh no! With you, yes indeed, to the altar I'll go!

The "Widow" is in the middle, the others in a circle around her. Everyone holds hands and sings the chorus to her while circling in one direction. On the verse, which is her solo, she taps three children as she sings "With you, I might...etc." and they circle in the other direction. The last one tapped is the next "widow" (or "widower") and the song is repeated until everyone has had a turn.

Doña Ana

Columbian

G   D⁷
Here we go a-walking where herbs grew all around;

             G   D⁷   G
See Doña Ana eating green parsley she has found.
Vamos a la vuelta del todo toronjil;
A ver a Doña Ana comiendo perejil.

All the children join hands in a circle except one in the center chosen by the group to be Doña Ana. They skip around her as they sing each verse. After singing the above verse:

They ask:
How are you Doña Ana?

Using appropriate gestures, Doña Ana says:
I have a headache.

The children sing:
Ana is not here now,
She's where her garden grows;
She's closing the carnation;
She's opening the rose.

They say:
How are you, Doña Ana?

With gestures, Doña Ana says:
I have a toothache.

The children sing:
Plates all made so golden,
And rims of crystal, too;
Let open and let close now,
The door we all go through.

They say:
How are you, Doña Ana?

With gestures, Doña Ana says:
I have a stomach ache.

Doña Ana sings:
Who are all these people,
A-going by this way?
They never let me slumber,
At night or in the day.

The children sing:
We are only students,
A-traveling afar;
To study at the chapel,
Of the Virgin of Pilar.

They say:
How are you, Doña Ana?

Doña Ana says:
I am dying.

All the children scatter with Doña Ana chasing them. The first one she catches becomes Doña Ana in playing the game again.

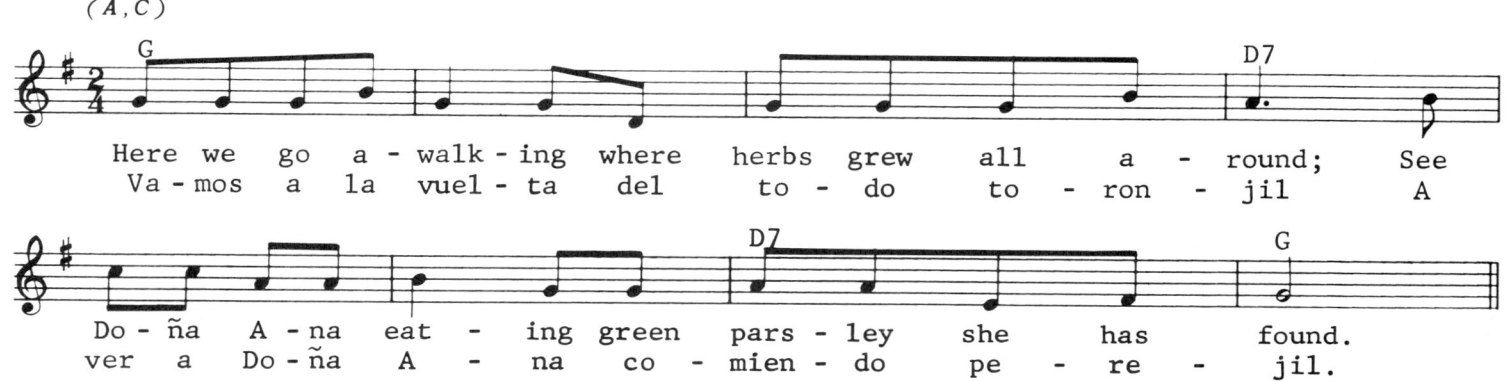

34

Matarile

Puerto Rican

```
   E        A      F#m    B⁷   E
1. Ambos todos, Matarile, rile, rile,          You and I together.

              F#        B⁷   E
   Ambos todos, Matarile, rile, ron.
```

2. Qué quiere usted?   What do you want?

3. Yo quiero-un páje.   I want a boy (page-boy).

4. Qué clase páje?   What kind of boy?

5. Quiero (name of child).   I want (name of child).

6. Qué oficio le pondremos?   What kind of work should he/she do?

7. Le pondremos maestra.   He/she should be a teacher.

8. Ella (él) dice que no le gusta.   She (he) says she doesn't like that one.

9. Le pondremos doctór.   She should be a doctor.

10. Ella dice que sí le gusta.   She says she likes that one.

11. Celebremos todos juntos.   Let us celebrate together.

My 5th grade Puerto Rican students taught me this singing game: all the players are lined up holding hands with one person across from them. That one is Matarile. Matarile sings the first verse while taking four steps toward the line of children, four back, four forward and four back. The line answers with the second verse, also taking four steps forward and back twice. Matarile does verse three, then verse four, Matarile five, the line six, Matarile seven and then the person who she's called for decides whether they want the occupation she's named. If they like it they do verse ten and they cross over to Matarile's side as they're singing. Then everyone does the last verse together by joining hands and skipping in a circle. Then Matarile starts again with her first choice at her side and the game continues until everyone has crossed over. If the person she's chosen doesn't like the occupation she names for him, he uses verse eight and then Matarile and her line have to name another occupation that will appeal.
Here are some more occupations to use:

abogado	lawyer	**secretaria**	secretary
carpentero	carpenter	**empleado**	clerk
matador	bullfighter	**contador**	accountant
enferma	nurse	**trabajador**	worker
músico	musician	**bombero**	fireman
político	politician	**cantor**	singer
policia	policeman	**dentmsta**	dentist

Fun Songs
for the Little Ones.

"We Whooped and We Hollered"

Some of these songs you will want to sing to the children in place of story-time. There was always one sure-fire method to gain the immediate and rapt attention of every child in the classroom: I would place my chair at the back of the room, take out my guitar and suggest that they bring their chairs (quietly) to where I was sitting so that I could *sing* them a story about a boy named Peter, (Peter Pong) or a girl named Tinya (I Wonder, I Wonder, I Wonder).

Other songs in this section you will want to teach them so that they can sing them to you. All are fun and all are perfect for Assemblies as well as the Classroom whether you want to sing them as a solo or get the children involved in singing them. Even when you are singing alone, a song you want them to hear, these are the kinds of songs that involve total participation. You will find yourself responding, as you sing, to the looks on their faces, which in turn are responding to your singing. A few of the songs in this section are perfect for a selected chorus.

Beans In My Ears

Len H. Chandler Jr.

    E
My mommy said not to put beans in my ears,

B⁷   E
Beans in my ears, beans in my ears,

    Em
My mommy said not to put beans in my ears,

B⁷   E
Beans in my ears.

Now why would I want to put beans in my ears,
Beans in my ears, beans in my ears?
Oh, why would I want to put beans in my ears,
Beans in my ears?

You can't hear your teachers with beans in your ears, etc.

Oh, maybe it's fun to have beans in your ears, etc.

Hey, Charlie, let's go and put beans in our ears, etc.

(Shouted) WHAT'S THAT YOU SAY? Let's put beans in our ears, etc.

YOU'LL HAVE TO SPEAK UP! I've got beans in my ears, etc.

Hey, Mommy, I've gone and put beans in my ears, etc.

That's nice, Son, just don't put those beans in your ears, etc.

I think that all grown-ups have beans in their ears, etc.

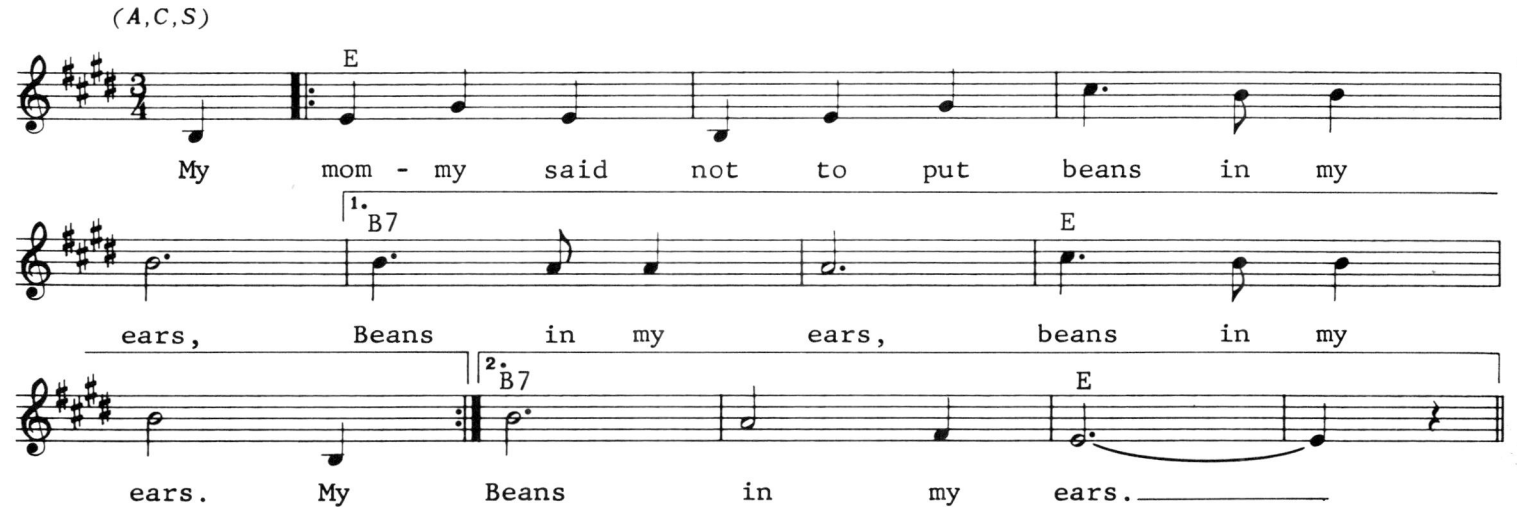

37

Little Brand New Baby

Tom Paxton

Chorus:

A   D   A
Hey, little brand new baby!

                          E   E⁷
Your momma and your daddy think you're mighty nice.

A   D   A
Hey, little brand new baby!

 A   E   A
I Hope you have a mighty nice life.

A   D
Your daddy's lookin' might proud,

A   E
Handin' out cigars all around the town,

A   D
Grinnin' like a possum and I think he's gonna crow,

     A   E⁷   A
And I hope you have a mighty nice life.

Your mama waited quite a while,
Carried you around for half a million miles,
But you know it was worth it when you look at her smile,
And I hope you have a mighty nice life.

It all lies ahead of you, and from this day,
It won't be easy as you travel your way,
But here's to your birth and I just want to say,
That I hope you have a mighty nice life.

(A,C,S)

Chorus:

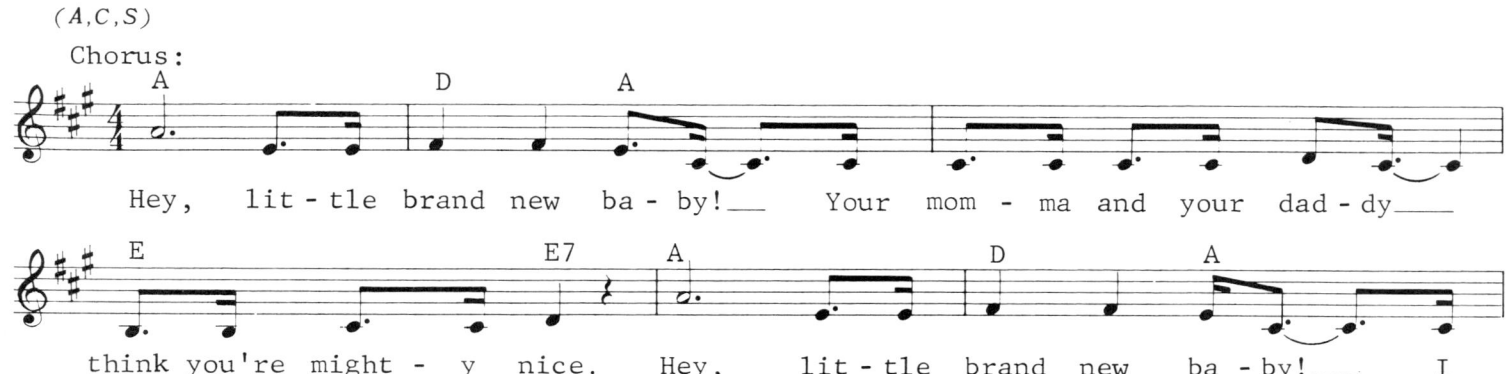

38

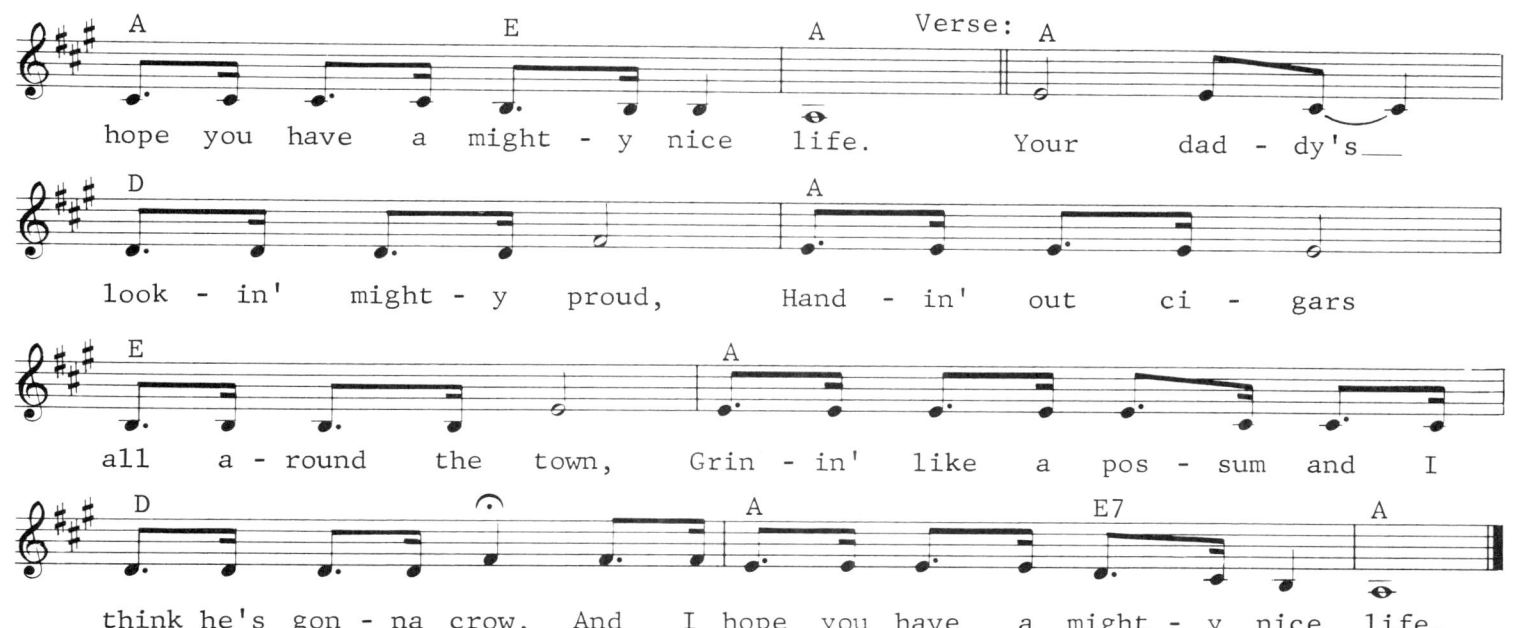

A E A Verse: A
hope you have a might - y nice life. Your dad - dy's
D A
look - in' might - y proud, Hand - in' out ci - gars
E A
all a - round the town, Grin - in' like a pos - sum and I
D A E7 A
think he's gon - na crow, And I hope you have a might - y nice life.

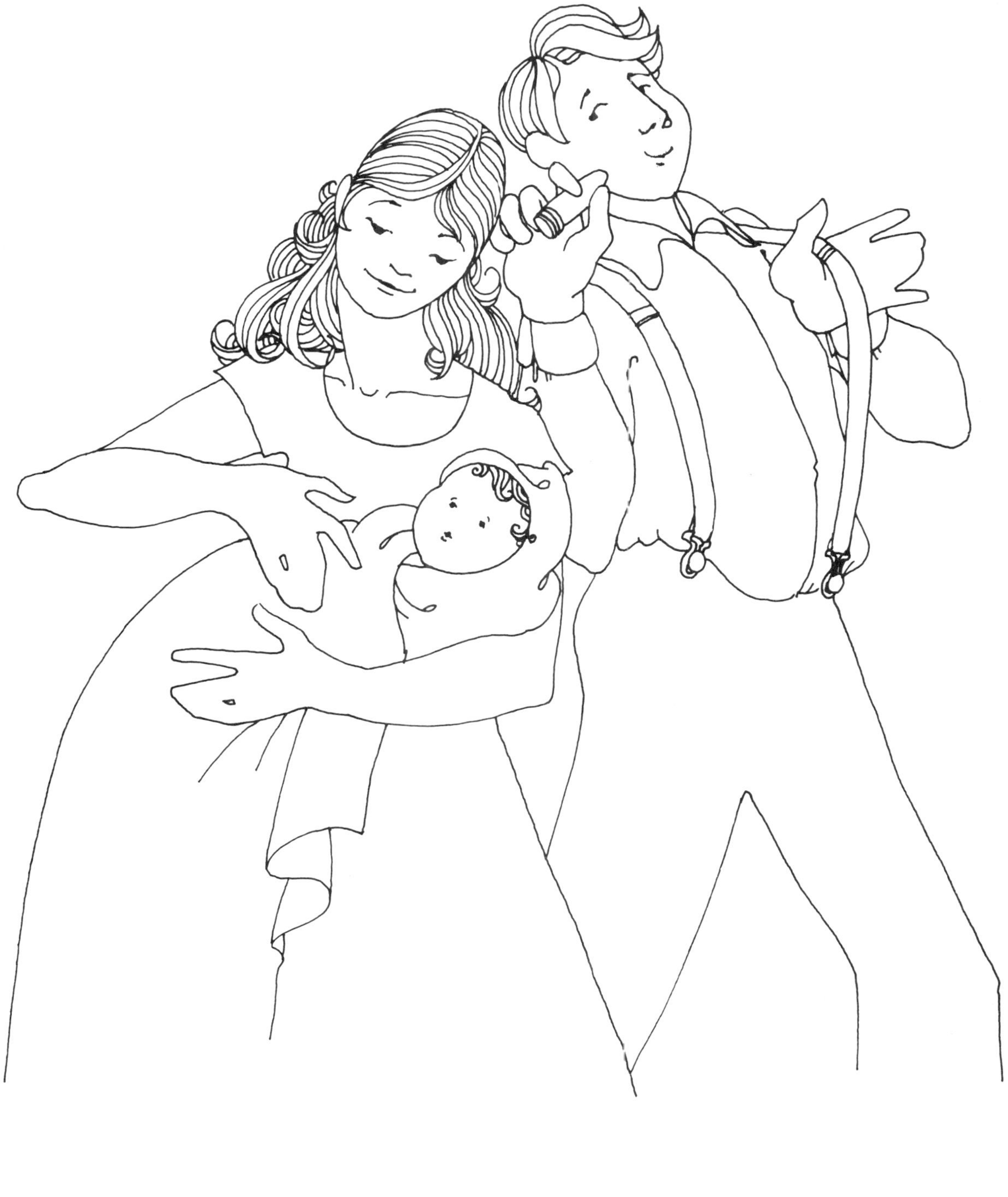

I Wonder, I Wonder, I Wonder

Pete Seeger

Chorus:

```
 C                     D
I wonder, I wonder, I wonder,

    G⁷                         C
What (child's name) can possibly do?

                     D
I wonder, I wonder, I wonder,

    G⁷               C
What Tinya can possibly do?
```

```
She can play with her blocks,

  D                          G⁷
Or go throw some rocks, climb a tree,

               C
And look at the view,

                   D
I wonder, I wonder, I wonder,

    G⁷               C
What Tinya can possibly do?
```

I see someone's hand,
I see someone's hair,
I hear someone say "peekaboo!"
I wonder, I wonder, I wonder, etc.

She crawls on the floor,
She looks 'round the door,
She's tryin' to put on my shoe,
I wonder, I wonder, I wonder, etc.

I see someone's foot,
I see someone's toe,
But I can't guess possibly who,
I wonder, I wonder, I wonder, etc.

(A,C,S)

Chorus:

I won-der, I won-der, I won-der,_____ What Tin-ya can pos-si-bly do?_____ I won-der, I won-der, I won-der,_____ What Tin-ya can pos-si-bly do._____ She can play with her blocks Or go throw some rocks, climb a tree And look at the view,_____ I won-der, I won-der, I won-der,_____ What Tin-ya can pos-si-bly do?_____

Don't You Push Me Down

Woody Guthrie
Tune: *Jingle Bells*

Chorus:

G
Don't you push me, push me, push me,

Don't you push me down.

C   G
Don't you push me, push me, push me,

D⁷   G
Don't you push me down!

G   C
You can play with me and you can hold my hand,

                D⁷   G
And you can comb my hair and you can ride my horse.

                      C
You can roll my ball and ride my 'trike around,

          D   D⁷   G
You can even laugh at me but don't you push me down!

You can play with me and you can dress my doll,
You can ride my scooter and you can ride my skates,
You can take my wagon and roll it around,
You can even get mad at me but don't you push me down!

You can play with me, we can play all day,
You can use my dishes if you'll put them away,
You can feed me apples and oranges and some plums,
You can even wash my face but don't you push me down!

Chorus:

G

Don't you push me, push me, push me, Don't you push me down.

C   **G**   **D7**   **G**

Don't you push me, push me, push me, Don't you push me down!

Verse:

You can play with me and you can hold my hand, And

D7   **C**

you can comb my hair and you can ride my horse.

C

You can roll my ball and ride my 'trike a - round,

D   **D7**   **G**

You can e - ven laugh at me but don't you push me down!

Mail Myself To You

Woody Guthrie

Chorus:

D   G A⁷
I'm gonna wrap myself in paper,

D   A
I'm gonna daub myself with glue,

D   G
Stick some stamps on top of my head,

A   D
I'm gonna mail myself to you!

When you see me in your mailbox,
Cut the string and let me out,
Wash the glue off of my fingers,
Stick some bubblegum in my mouth!

           A⁷
I'm gonna tie me up in a red string,

D   A
I'm gonna tie blue ribbons, too,

D   G A⁷
I'm gonna climb up in my mailbox,

D   A D
I'm gonna mail myself to you!

Take me out of my wrapping paper,
Wash the stamps off of my head,
Pour me full of ice cream sodies,
Put me in my nice warm bed.

Never Argue With A Bee

Malvina Reynolds

Chorus:

C
Never argue with a bee,

G⁷
He has got a stingaree.

Be he worker, be he drone,

          C
You had best leave him alone.

F
He has got his work to do,

C
Getting honey from the tree,

                G⁷
If you know what's good for you,

          C
Do not argue with a bee.

Well, a hornet knows his rights,
And it hurts when he alights.
You will surely get your lumps,
Cause his stinger, it is trumps.

And the wasp is very wild,
If you bother with his child.
Let him go where he is bound,
Do not try to mess around.

You can get along with bees,
Call them mister, ask them please,
Let them work and be content,
But avoid the argument.

There Was A Man
(And He Was Mad)

Mary O. Eddy
From *American Folk Songs for Children* by Ruth Crawford Seeger
Copyright 1939
Reprinted by Permission of Doubleday & Company, Inc.
All Rights Reserved

```
      E           A      E
There was a man and he was mad,

              B⁷      E
And he jumped into a pudding bag.
```

The pudding bag it was so fine,
That he jumped into a bottle of wine.

The bottle of wine it was so clear,
That he jumped into a bottle of beer.

The bottle of beer it was so thick,
That he jumped into a walking stick.

The walking stick it was so narrow,
That he jumped into a wheel barrow.

The wheel barrow it did so crack,
That he jumped onto a horse's back.

The horse's back it did so break,
That he jumped into a chocolate cake.

The chocolate cake became so rotten,
That he jumped into a bag of cotton.

The bag of cotton it caught on fire,
And blew him up to Jeremiah. Poof! Poof! Poof!

Marty

Malvina Reynolds

A   E⁷ A

Move over and make room for *(child's name),*

  D   A

He doesn't take very much space,

  D   A

Since Marty is one of our very best friends,

  E⁷   A

We surely can find him a place.

Chorus:

    D   A   E⁷   A

Move over, move over, and quick like a riggitty jig,

    D   A   E⁷   A

We'll always move over for Marty, for Marty is not very big.

He won't have to stand in the corner,
He won't have to sit on the floor,
For we can move over for Marty,
And still there is room for one more.

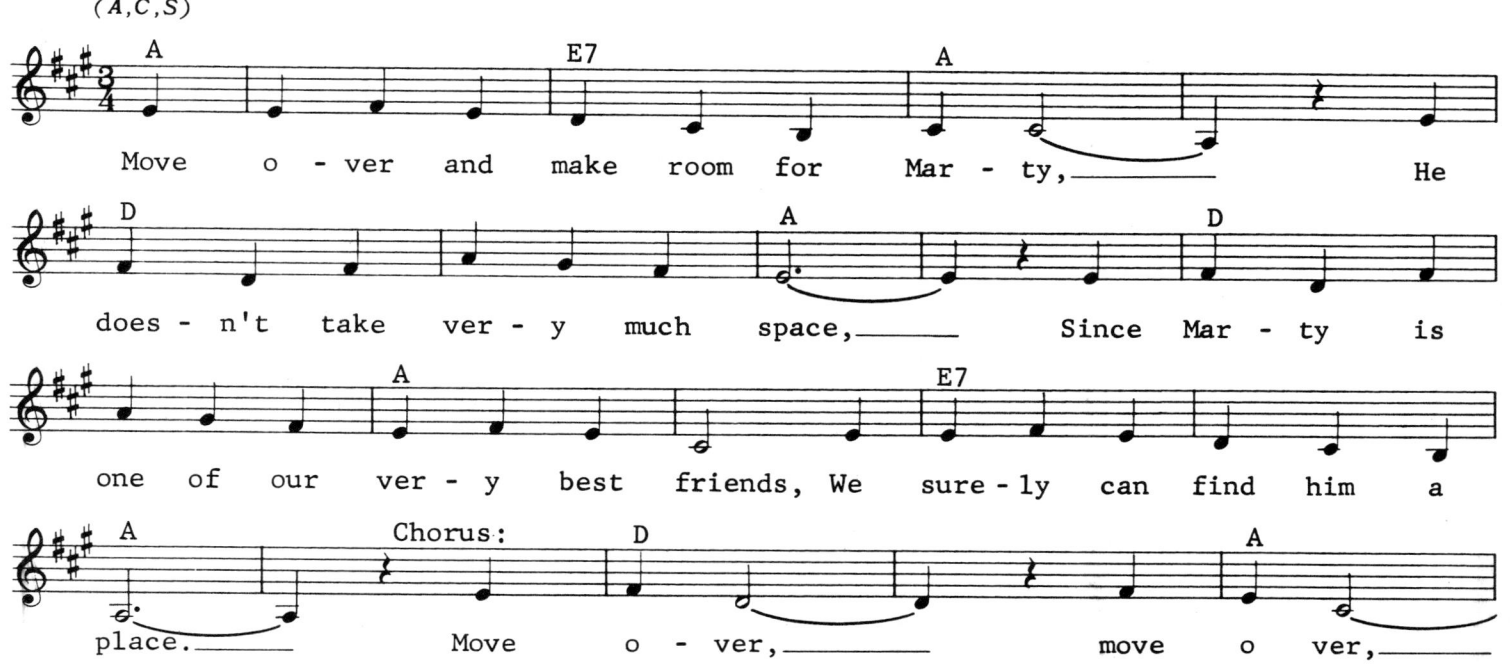

and quick like a rig - gi - ty jig,

We'll al - ways move o - ver for Mar - ty,

for Mar - ty is not ver - y big.

Birthday Hallelujah

Malvina Reynolds

```
A           E⁷        A              E
Who's the little what-not came along our way,

D     A     E⁷             A
Nancy, Nancy, fourteen years to-day!*

A                    E⁷      A                 E
Looked around the kitchen, thought she'd better stay,

D     A     E⁷             A
Nancy, Nancy, fourteen years to-day!
```

Chorus:

```
D                    A
Sing Hallelujah and wave the soup tureen,

E⁷          A
Hold your hat, hold your specs,

B⁷            E
Man the pumps, clear the decks,

D              A        E⁷        A
Lord knows what will happen next, Nancy's fourteen!
```

Landed on the chimney, or maybe in the hay,
Nancy, Nancy, fourteen years today!
Looked the family over, gave a mild okay,
Nancy, Nancy, fourteen years today!

Final Chorus:
Sing Hallelujah and shake the tambourine,
Watch your clothes, watch your toes,
Here she comes, there she goes,
Where she stops nobody knows, Nancy's fourteen!

Optional Choruses:
Sing Hallelujah and wave the other shoe...Stevie is two.
Sing Hallelujah and bang the garden gate...Julie is eight.
Sing Hallelujah and shinny up a tree...Bobby is three.

*Substitute names of children in your group.

50

(A, C, S)

Who's the lit-tle what-not came a-long our way, Nan - cy,

Nan - cy, four-teen years to-day! Looked a-round the kitch-en,

thought she'd bet-ter stay, Nan - cy, Nan cy, four-teen years to -

Chorus:

- day! Sing Hal-le-lu-jah and wave the soup tu-reen,

Hold your hat, hold your specs, Man the pumps, clear the decks,

Lord knows what will hap-pen next, Nan - cy's four - teen!

Declaration of Independence

Wolcott Gibbs and Celius Dougherty

      G
He will just do nothing at all,

                  D⁷   G
He will just sit there in the noonday sun,

And when they speak to him, he will not answer them,

             Em
Because he does not wish to.

G
And when they tell him to eat his dinner,

He will just laugh at them,

            Em
And he will not take his nap,

Because he does not care to.

G   D⁷   G
He will just sit there in the noonday sun,

He will go away and play with the panda,

And when they come to look for him,

           Em
He will stick them with spears,

                           G
And put them in the garbage and put the cover on.

And he will not go out in the fresh air,

Nor eat his veg'tables,

                  Em
And he will grow thin as a marble.

             G
He will just do nothing at all,

                  D⁷   G
He will just sit there in the noonday sun.

52

All Work Together

Woody Guthrie

Chorus:

B⁷   E   B⁷
So we all work together with a wiggle and a giggle,

    E   B⁷   E
We all work together with a giggle and a grin,

With a wiggle and a giggle and a google and a woggle,

                         B⁷   E
A jigger and a jagger and a giggle and a grin.

    B⁷
My mama said, and my teacher, too,

                   E
All kinds of work that I can do,

B⁷
Dry my dishes, sweep my floor,

        E   A   E
But if we all work together, well, it won't take long.

My daddy said, and my grandpa, too,
There's work, worka-work for me to do,
Paint my fence, mow my lawn,
And if we all work together it shouldn't take long.

My sister said and my brother too,
Lots and lotsa work that I can do,
I can bring her candy, and I can bring him gum,
But if we work together we won't take long.

I tell my mommy and my daddy too,
I tell my grandma and grandpa too,
I tell my sister and my brother too,
There's lots and lots of work to do,
You can bring me pennies and candy and gum,
But if we work together
It won't take long!

(A,C,S)

Chorus:

B7 · E · · · · · · · · · · B7

So we all work to-geth-er with a wig-gle and a gig-gle,— We

E · · · · · B7 · · · · E ·

all work to-geth-er with a gig-gle and a grin. With a

· · · · · · · · · · · · · · · · ·

wig-gle and a gig-gle and a goo-gle and a woo-gle, A

· · · · · · · B7 · · · E · Verse:

jig-ger and a jag-ger and a gig-gle and a grin. My

B7 · · · · · · · · · · · · ·

ma-ma said and my teach-er, too, All kinds of work that

· · · · E · B7 · · · · · · · ·

I can do: Dry my dish-es,____ sweep my floor, But if we

E · · · A · · · · E · · ·

all work to-geth-er, well, it won't take long.

55

The Marvelous Toy

Tom Paxton

```
        D           A⁷              D            A⁷
When I was just a wee little lad, and full of health and joy,

    G           D              E⁷       A⁷
My father homeward came one night, and gave to me a toy.

    D         A⁷          D    G    D
A wonder to behold it was, with many colors bright,

        G             D           A⁷    E⁷      A⁷
And the moment I laid my eyes on it, it became my hearts delight.
```

Chorus:

```
        D                        A⁷                  D        G    D
It went "Zip" when it moved and "Bop" when it stopped and "Whirr" when it stood still,

    G         D           A⁷         D
I never knew just what it was and I guess I never will.
```

The first time that I picked it up I had a big surprise,
For right on its bottom were two big buttons that looked like big green eyes.
I first pushed one and then the other, and then I twisted its lid,
And when I set it down again, here is what it did:

It first marched left and then marched right and then marched under a chair,
And when I looked where it had gone, it wasn't even there!
I started to sob and my daddy laughed, for he knew that I would find,
When I turned around, my marvelous toy, chugging from behind.

Well, the years have gone by too quickly, it seems, and I have my own little boy,
And yesterday I gave to him my marvelous little toy.
His eyes nearly popped right out of his head and he gave a squeal of glee,
Neither one of us knows just what it is, but he loves it, just like me.

Last Chorus:
It still goes "Zip" when it moves and "Bop" when it stops,
And "Whirr" when it stands still,
I never knew just what it was,
And I guess I never will.

Tingle Lay O!

Jamaican

Chorus:

A   D   A E⁷   A
Tingle Lay O! Come little donkey, come.

A   D   A E⁷   A
Tingle Lay O! Come little donkey, come.

        D   A
My donkey eat, my donkey sleep, my donkey

E⁷   A
Kick with his two hind feet. (2x)

My donkey walk, my donkey talk, my donkey
Eat with a spoon and fork. (2x)

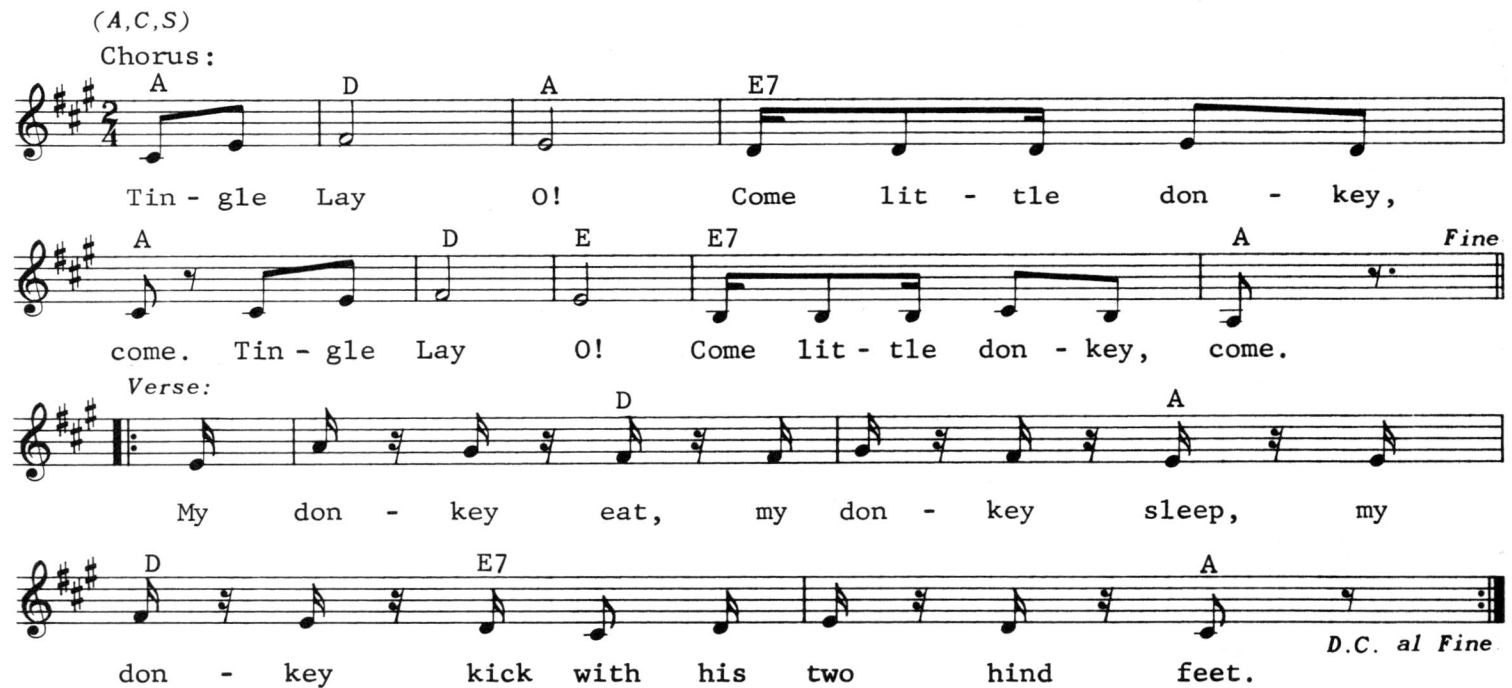

I Had A Little Rooster

North American

C
I had a little rooster and my rooster pleased me,

G⁷
I fed my rooster on a green berry tree,

C   F   C
And my little rooster went "Cock-a-doodle-doo-lee—

G⁷   C
Doodle-ee-doodle-ee-doodle-ee-doo!"

I had a little hen and my hen pleased me,
I fed my hen on a green berry tree,
And my little hen went "Cluck! Cluck! Cluck!"
And my little rooster went "Cock-a-doodle-doo-lee—
Doodle-ee-doodle-ee-doodle-ee-doo!"

I had a little duck, etc.   Cat, etc.
I fed my duck, etc.   Cow, etc.
And my little duck went "Quack! Quack! Quack!"   Pig, etc.
And my little hen went, etc.   Baby, etc.

And, of course, this song goes on as long as the children can keep adding the names of animals.

Jig Along Home

Woody Guthrie

Chorus:

E   B⁷
Jig, jig-a jig, jig, jig along home,

                     E
Jig, jig-a jig, jig, jig along home.

                   A
Jig along, jig along, jig along home,

B⁷   E
Jig, jig-a jig along, jig along home.

      E   B⁷
Well, I went to the dance and the animals come,

            E
Jay-bird danced with horse-shoes on,

Grasshopper danced till he fell to the floor,

B⁷   E
Jig along, jig along, jig along home.

Well the fish warmed up the fishing reel,
Lobster danced on the peacock's tail.
Baboon danced with the rising moon,
Jig along, jig along, jig along home.

And the rooster cut his weevily wheat,
The catfish tromped the cuckoo's feet.
The ostrich stomped with the kangaroo,
Jig along, jig along, jig along home.

And the mama rat took off her hat,
Shook the house with the old tom cat.
The alligator beat his tail on the drum,
Jig along, jig along, jig along home.

The boards did rattle and the house did shake,
The clouds they laughed and the world did quake.
New moon rattled some silver spoons,
Jig along, jig along, jig along home.

The nails flew loose and the floor broke down,
Everybody danced around and around.
The house came down and the crowd went home,
Jig along, jig along, jig along home.

(A,C,S)

Chorus:

Jig, jig - a jig, jig, Jig a - long home, Jig, jig - a jig, jig,

Jig a-long home. Jig a - long, jig a - long, Jig a - long home,

Jig, jig - a jig a-long, Jig a-long home. Well, I went to the dance and the

Verse:

an - i - mals come; Jay - bird danced with horse - shoes on;

Grass - hop - per danced till he fell to the floor,

Jig a - long, jig a - long, Jig a - long home.

We Whooped And We Hollered

English

```
         G              Em              D⁷
We whooped and we hollered and the first thing we did find,

        G           Em     D⁷
Was a barn on the hill and that we left behind,

          D     G
Look-a there now.

                     Em   D⁷
Some said it was a barn, some said, "Nay,"

        G          Em              D⁷
Some said it was a church with the steeple cut away,

          D     G
Look-a there now.
```

We whooped and we hollered and the thing that we did find,
Was a pig in a lane and that we left behind,
Look-a there now.
Some said it was a pig, some said, "Nay,"
Some said it was an elephant with his trunk cut away,
Look-a there now.

We whooped and we hollered, etc.
Was a pig in a lane, etc.
Look-a there now.
Some said it was the moon in the tree, some said, "Nay,"
Some said it was a cheese with it's half cut away,
Look-a there now.

We whooped and we hollered, etc.
Was a pig in a lane, etc.
Some said it was a frog in the well, some said, "Nay,"
Some said it was a jaybird with its feathers plucked away,
Look-a there now.

We whooped and we hollered, etc.
Was a pig in a lane, etc.
Some said it was an owl in the tree, some said, "Nay,"
Some said it was a bogeyman and so we ran away,
Look-a there now.

Rumor has it that this song has sometimes been used to show how truth may be in the eye of the beholder and objective observation may be subjective opinion. However it is used, the children have a great deal of fun with it.

(A,C,S)

We whooped and we hol-lered and the first thing we did find, Was a barn on a hill__ and that we left be-hind,__ Look-a there now. Some said it was a barn, some said "Nay," Some said it was a church__ with the stee-ple cut a-way,__ Look-a there now.

The Keeper

English

```
        A                D      A
The keeper would a-hunting go,

                          D        A
And under his coat he carried a bow,

All for to shoot at a merrie little doe,

   D         E⁷              A
Among the leaves so green, O!
```

Chorus:

```
¹A          ²          ¹
Jackie boy! Master! Sing ye well?

²           ¹           ²
Very well. Hey down! Ho down!

All

D         E⁷    A     D      E⁷   A
Derry derry down! Among the leaves so green, O!

¹                        ²
To my Hey, down, down! To my Ho, down, down!

¹           ²
Hey down! Ho down!

All

D         E⁷    A     D      E⁷ A
Derry derry down! Among the leaves so green, O!
```

The first doe she did cross the plain,
The keeper fetched her back again,
Where she is now she may remain
Among the leaves so green, O!

The second doe she cross'd the brook,
The keeper fetched her back with his hook,
Where she is now you may go and look,
Among the leaves so green, O!

This is a response song on the Chorus.

The Weavers never liked the doe being killed so they added the following verses:

The first doe she did cross the plain
The keeper fetched her back again
Where she is now she may remain
Among the leaves so green, O!

The next doe she did cross the brook
The keeper fetched her back with his hook
Where she is now you may go look
Among the leaves so green, O!

The keeper did a-hunting go
In the woods he caught a doe
She looked so sad that he had to let her go
Among the leaves so green, O!

I Love An Old Lady
(The Old Woman Who Swallowed A Fly)

Rose Bonne and Alan Mills

G
I know an old woman who swallowed a fly,

A⁷   D⁷
I don't know why she swallowed the fly,

                    G
I guess she'll die!

G
I know an old woman who swallowed a spider,

        A⁷   D⁷
That wiggled and jiggled and tiggled inside her.

            G
She swallowed the spider to catch the fly,

A⁷   D⁷
I don't know why she swallowed the fly,

                    G
I guess she'll die!

G
I know an old woman who swallowed a bird,

A⁷   D⁷
How absurd! To swallow a bird!

        G
She swallowed the bird to catch the spider,

        A⁷   D⁷
Who wiggled and jiggled and tiggled inside her,

            G
She swallowed the spider to catch the fly,

    A⁷   D⁷
I don't know why she swallowed the fly,

                    G
I guess she'll die!

I know an old woman who swallowed a cat,
Imagine that, to swallow a cat.
She swallowed the cat to catch the bird,
She swallowed the bird to catch the spider, etc.

I know an old woman who swallowed a dog,
Wasn't she a hog, to swallow a dog?
She swallowed the dog to catch the cat, etc.

I know an old woman who swallowed a goat,
Just opened her throat, and swallowed a goat.
She swallowed the goat to catch the dog, etc.

I know an old woman who swallowed a cow,
I don't know how, she swallowed a cow.
She swallowed a cow to catch the goat, etc.

I know an old woman who swallowed a rhinoceros,
How preposerous, to swallow a rhinoceros, etc.

I know an old woman who swallowed a horse,
Swallowed a horse, swallowed a horse.
She's dead, of course!

(A,C,S)

I know an old wom-an who swal-lowed a fly,

I don't know why she swal-lowed the fly, I guess she'll die!

I know an old wom-an who swal-lowed a spi-der, That

wig-gled and jig-gled and tig-gled in-side her. She

swal-lowed the spi-der to catch the fly, I don't know why she

swal-lowed the fly, I guess she'll die! I

know an old wom-an who swal-lowed a bird, how ab-surd! To

swal-low a bird! She swal-lowed the bird to catch the spi-der, Who

wig-gled and jig-gled and tig-gled in-side her, She

swal-lowed the spi-der to catch the fly,

I don't know why she swal-lowed the fly, I guess she'll die!

Peter Pong

Johnny Richardson

```
    E    B⁷      E               B⁷   E
There was a boy named Peter, his name was Peter Pong,

        B⁷      E    A       E      B⁷   E
They always called him Peter Ping, but his name was Peter Pong.

        B⁷       E                      B⁷       E
He went to play some ping pong with friends who lived so near,

        B⁷     E     A    E   B⁷      E
And ev'ry time his mother called, this is what you'd hear:
```

Chorus:

```
E   B⁷  E       B⁷   E
Ping! Pong! Ping! Ping! Pong! Ping!

              B⁷        E  A E          B⁷      E
With a ping pong paddle and ball he couldn't hear his mother call,

           B⁷    E     A      E      B⁷        E
'Cause he's so dizzy from bein' so busy with a ping pong paddle and ball.

    B⁷  E      B⁷   E
Ping! Pong! Ping! Ping! Pong! Ping!
```

One morning he played hookey and he didn't go to school,
And he knew very very well that it was against the rule,
So his mother went to find him, she called but not a word,
She just kept walking up and down and suddenly she heard:

So she caught him by the hand and led him back to school,
And the teacher sat him in a corner high upon a stool,
And when the school was over, he flew out like a bird
And over to his friends he went and what do you think we heard?

So his mother bought him a table, and a paddle and ball besides,
And when he came home from school one day there was a big surprise,
And now they come to his house, they come from far and near,
And anytime you pass his house, this is what you'd hear:

(A,C,S)

There was a boy named Pe - ter, his name was Pe - ter Pong, They al - ways called him Pe - ter Ping, but his name was Pe - ter Pong. He went to play some ping-pong with his friends who lived so near, And ev - 'ry time his moth-er called, this is what you'd hear:

Chorus:

Ping! Pong! Ping! Ping! Pong! Ping! With a ping - pong pad - dle and ball he could - n't hear his moth - er____ call, 'Cause he's so diz - zy from be - in' so bus - y with a ping-pong pad- dle and ball. Ping! Pong! Ping! Ping! Pong! Ping!

The Never Song

Edward Lipton

```
        D                         A⁷
I've heard a collie bark, I've heard a police dog bark,

                          D
I've heard a bulldog bark, I've heard a beagle bark,

                              G
I've heard a chihuahua bark, I've heard a poodle bark,

      D    A⁷       D
But I never heard a tree bark.
```

Chorus:

```
            A⁷
A tree bark, a tree bark,

                  D
But I've never heard a tree bark.
```

I've seen a pigeon fly, I've seen a bee fly,
I've seen a bat fly, I've seen an eagle fly,
I've seen a hawk fly, I've seen a sparrow fly,
But I never saw . . . A house fly
Chorus: A house fly, etc.

I've had head pains, I've had stomach pains,
I've had foot pains, I've had leg pains,
I've had back pains, I've had neck pains,
But I never had . . . window panes.
Chorus: Window panes, etc.

I have a door key, I have a car key,
I have a trunk key, I have a closet key,
I have a front door key, I have a back door key,
But I don't have . . . a monkey.
Chorus: A monkey, etc.

I've used a telephone dial, I've used a washing machine dial,
I've used a radio dial, I've used a television dial,
I've used a broiler dial, I've used a sun dial,
But I never used . . . a crocodile.
Chorus: A crocodile, etc.

I heard a man scream, I heard a boy scream,
I heard a woman scream, I heard a girl scream,
I heard a loud scream, I heard a louder scream,
But I never heard . . . an ice cream.
Chorus: An ice cream, etc.

(A,C,S,SC)

I've heard a col-lie bark, I've heard a po-

-lice dog bark, I've heard a bull-dog bark, I've heard a

bea-gle bark, I've heard a chi-hua-hua bark, I've heard a

Chorus:

poo-dle bark, But I nev-er heard _____ a tree bark. A

tree bark, a tree bark, But I've

nev-er heard _____ a tree bark.

The Sound Song

Edward Lipton

```
      D                     A⁷
The airplane it likes to go zoom, zoom, zoom,

                      D
The drum, it likes to go boom, boom, boom,

                       A⁷          G
The owl, he likes to go whom, whom, whom,

        A⁷
The rhinoceros  likes lots of room, room, room.
```

Chorus:

```
A⁷           D
Room, room, room, room,

       Am                 D
The rhinoceros  likes lots of room, room, room,

A⁷           D
Room, room, room, room,

       A⁷                   D
The rhinoceros  likes lots of room, room, room.
```


The kangaroo likes to go jump, jump, jump
The elephant likes to go thump, thump, thump
The camel he likes to go hump, hump, hump
The dinosaur likes to go clump, clump, clump.
Chorus: Clump, Clump, etc.

The lightning he likes to go flash, flash, flash
The thunder he likes to go crash, crash, crash
The water he likes to go splash, splash, splash
The potato he likes to go mash, mash, mash.
Chorus: Mash, mash, etc.

The snail he likes to go creep, creep, creep
The car he likes to go beep, beep, beep
The weeping willow likes to go weep, weep, weep
As for me I like to go sleep, sleep, sleep
Chorus: Sleep, sleep, etc.

Animal Song

Michigan

C   F
Alligator, hedgehog, anteater, bear,

G⁷   C
Rattlesnake, buffalo, anaconda hare.

Bullfrog, woodchuck, wolverine goose,
Whip-oorwill, chipmunk, jackal, moose.

Mud turtle, whale, glow-worm, bat,
Salamander, snail, Maltese cat.

Al li - ga - tor, hedge - hog, ant - eat - er, bear,

Rat - tle - snake, buf - fa - lo, an - a - con - da, hare.

The Spelling Song

Edward Lipton

D
If c-o-r-k spells cork

A   D
And f-o-r-k spells fork

G   S
And s-t-o-r-k spells stork,

A   D
Does w-o-r-k spell work?

Chorus:

G   A⁷   D
Words, words, words, words,

G   A⁷   D
How do you say all the words?

G   A⁷   D
Words, words, words, words,

A⁷   D
Sometimes it seems quite absurd.

If c-a-s-h spells cash
And d-a-s-h spells dash
And m-a-s-h spells mash,
Does w-a-s-h spell wash?*

If b-l-e-w spells blew
And f-l-e-w spells flew
And n-e-w spells new,
Does s-e-w spell sew?

If r-o-o-t spells root
And b-o-o-t spells boot
And h-o-o-t spells hoot,
Does f-o-o-t spell foot?

If l-o-v-e spells love
And d-o-v-e spells dove
And s-h-o-v-e spells shove,
Does m-o-v-e spell move?

*Note: Last word of fourth line of each verse should be pronounced to rhyme with the pronunciation of the last word of each of the preceding lines. Children should be given time to reply to the question at the end of each verse.

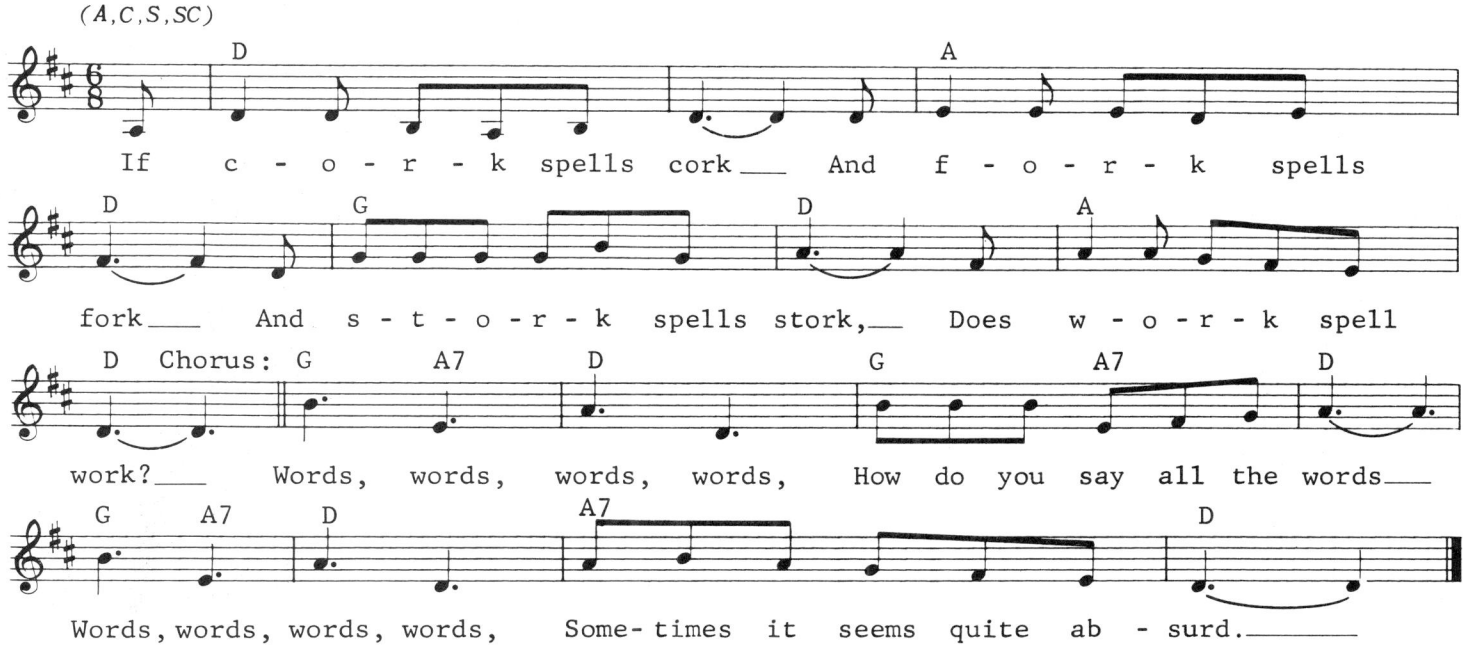

Three Little Piggies

Guy Carawan

     A   D   A
Oh, there was once a sow who had three little pigs,

A   A
Three little piggies had she.

     D   A
The old sow always went "Oink! Oink! Oink!

     E⁷   A
And the piggies went "Wheee! Wheee! Wheee!

Now, one day, one of those three little pigs,
To the other two piggies said he:
"Why don't we try to go 'Oink! Oink! Oink!'
Instead of going 'Wheee! Wheee! Wheee!'? "

Now those three little piggies grew skinny and lean,
Skinny they well might be.
For they always tried to go "Oink! Oink! Oink!"
Instead of going "Wheee! Wheee! Wheee!"

Now those three little piggies, they up and died,
A very sad sight to see.
So don't you ever try to go "Oink! Oink! Oink!"
When ya oughta go "Wheee! Wheee! Wheee!"

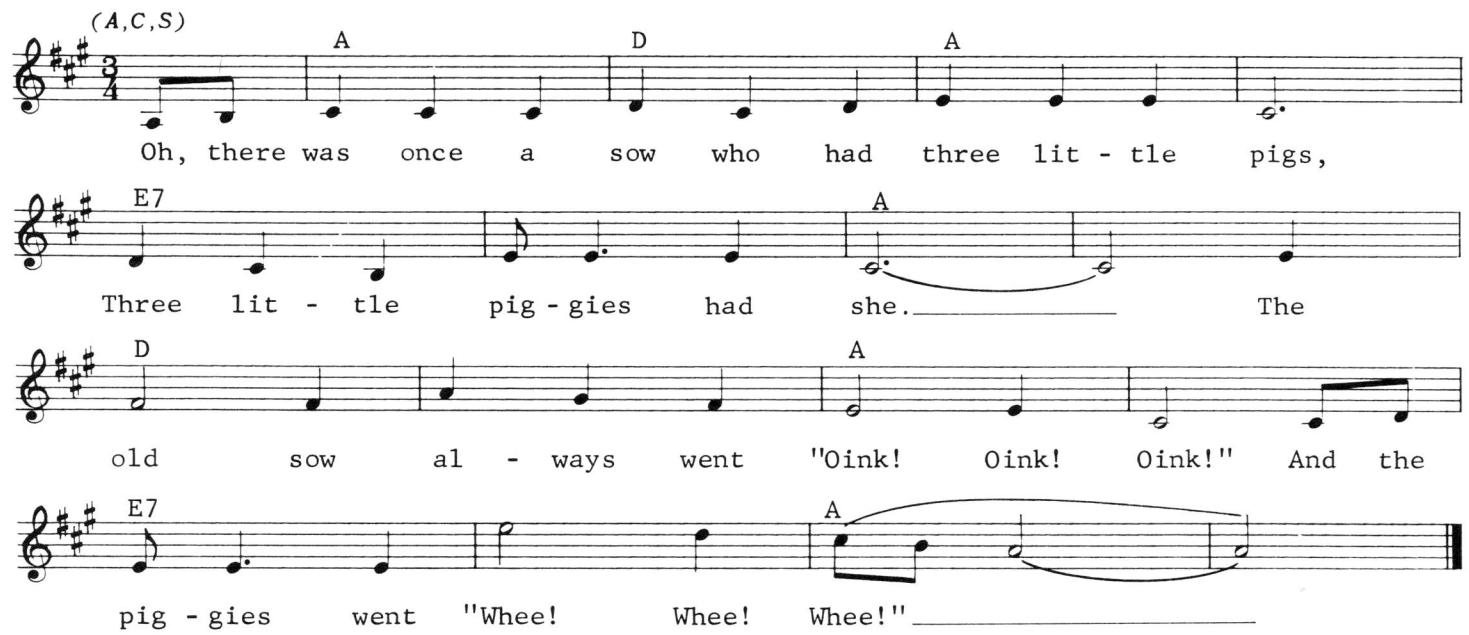

Three Craw

Scottish

```
A                       D       E⁷  A            D E⁷
Three craw sat upon a wa', sat upon a wa', sat upon a wa'-a-a-a, (wall)
A                              D      E⁷  A
Three craw sat upon a wa', on a cold and frosty morning.
```

The first craw could'na find his ma, etc.

The second one could'na find his pa, etc.

The third craw ate the other twa' (two) , etc.

The fourth craw was'na there ata' (at all) , etc.

And tha's a' I heer'd aboot the craw (that's all) , etc.

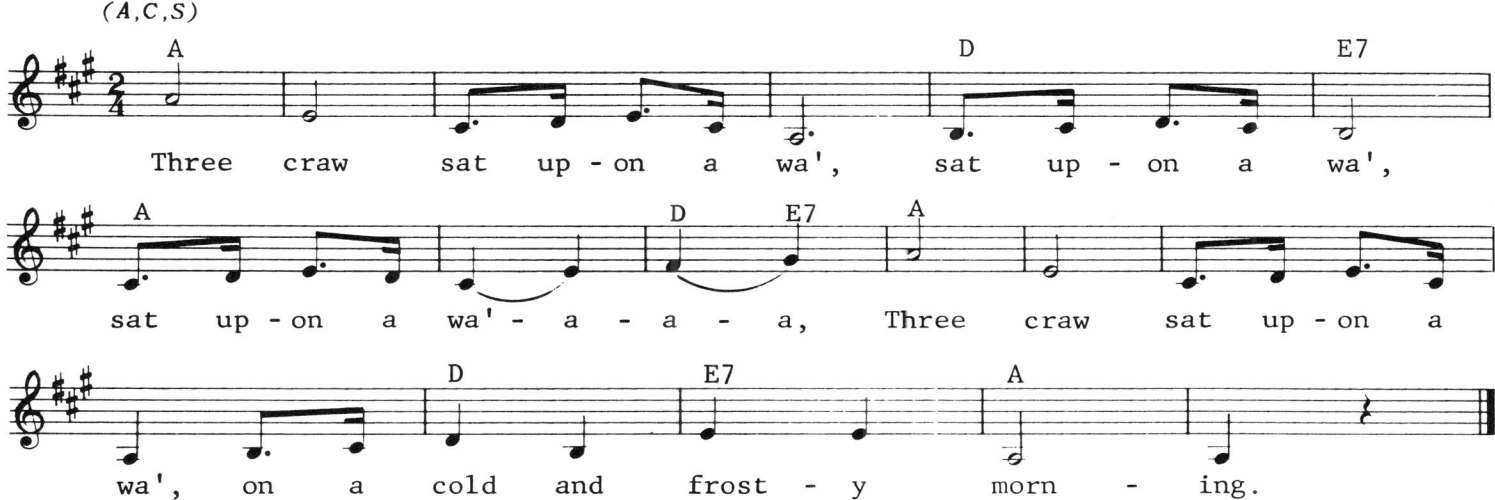

All The Colors Of The Rainbow

Edward Lipton

C   Em
There are blue skies and white clouds,

F   G⁷
And green grass and brown earth,

C   G⁷
And all of them together,

      C   G⁷   C
Blend in perfect harmony.

Chorus:

F   C
All the colors of the rainbow,

D⁷   G⁷
All the shades of light and dark,

Am   F   C
All the colors of the rainbow,

     F   G⁷   C
How beautiful they are.

There are red flowers and yellow flowers,
And blue flowers and white flowers,
But every flower is a gift of love,
And adds beauty to this world.

There are red birds and yellow birds,
And black birds and white birds,
But every bird has wings to fly,
And how high they all can fly.

There are red men and yellow men,
And white men and black men.
There are many men but every man,
Is a man just the same.

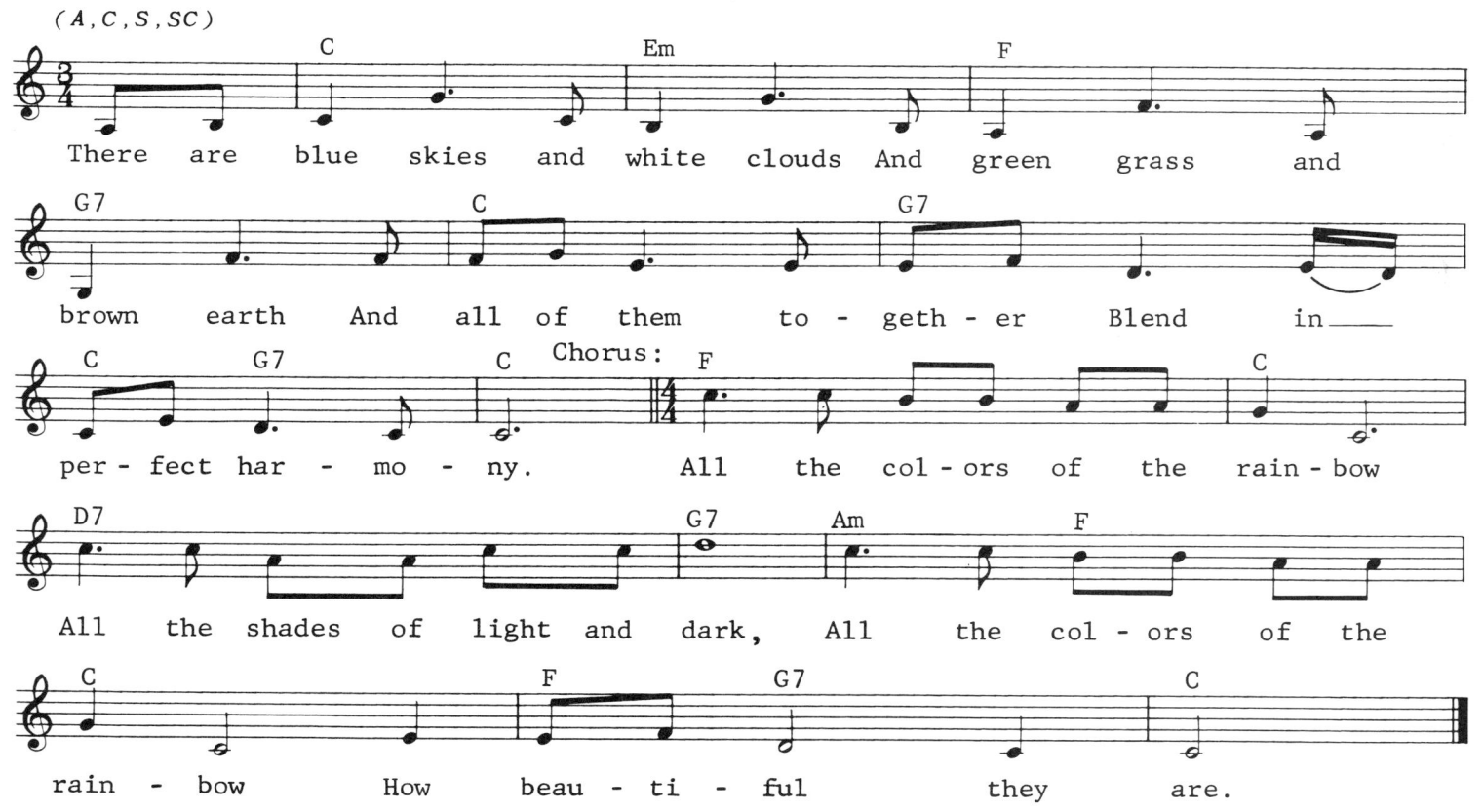

78

Put On Your Hat

Malvina Reynolds

```
D                 Em      D                       G  D
Put on your hat and come with me and let's go out in the garden,

G              D            A⁷                 D
We'll see the flowers shining bright, yellow and red and blue and white,

        G              D                  A⁷        D
And the bees buzz by and the butterflies fly where the pretty flowers grow.


Put on your hat and come with me and let's go down to the playground,
We'll see the children shining bright, yellow and tan and brown and white,
All in a ring or flying on the swing, where the pretty children grow.
```

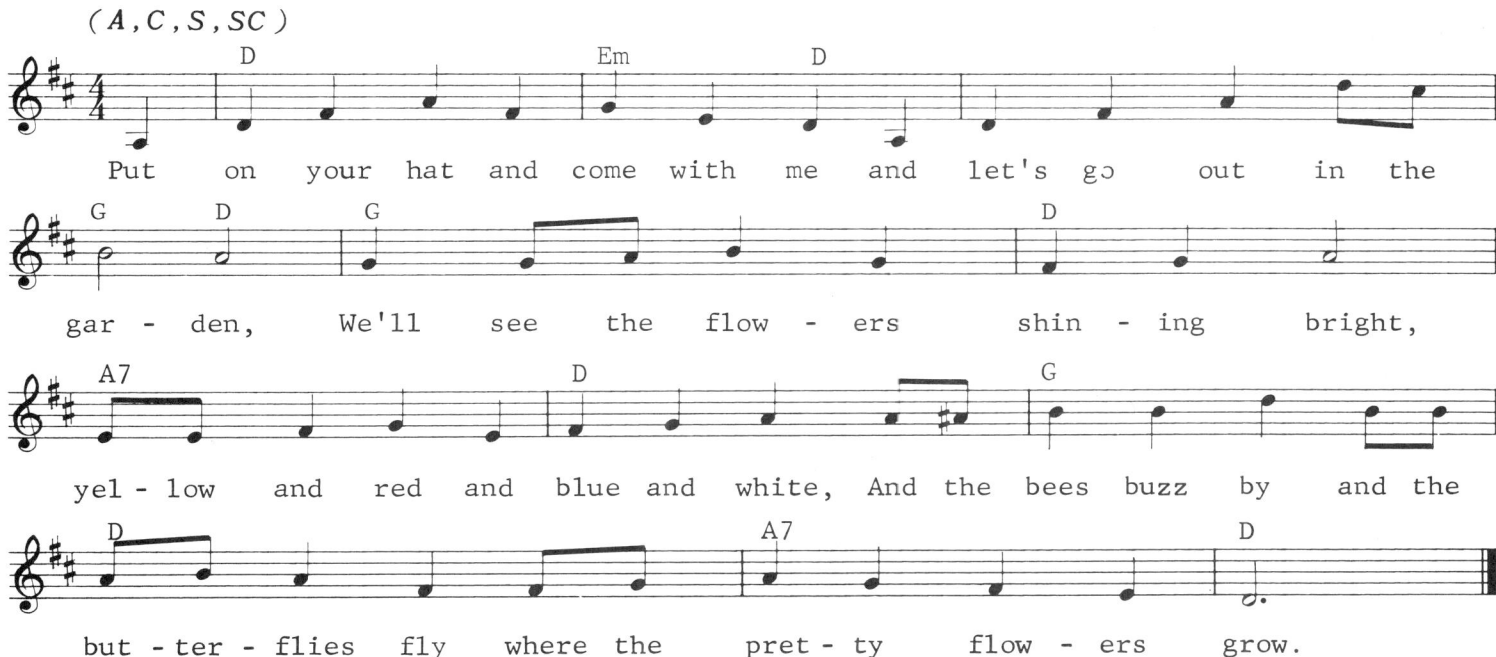

Land Of The Silver Birch

Canadian Indian

Em
Land of the silver birch, home of the beaver,

Am   **Em**
And where the mighty moose wanders at will.

Chorus:

                       E⁷
Blue lakes and rocky shores, I will return once more,

Em
Boom-diddy-um-bum, bum-bum.

Boom-diddy-um-bum, bum-bum.

High on a rocky ledge I'll build my wigwam,
Close by the water's edge silent and still.

Down in the forest glade deep in the lowlands,
My heart cries out for thee, Hills of the North.

While half the group continues repeating "Boom-diddy-um-bum, bum-bum" over and over again the other half sings the verse again. This is also a good song to add the rhythm instruments to.

The Little Boy And The Sheep

English

G   C   G   C⁷   D⁷   G
Lazy sheep pray tell me why, in the pleasant fields you lie,

C   D⁷   C   A⁷   D D⁷
Eating grass and daisies white, from the morning to the night,

G   C   G   C⁷   D⁷   G
Ev'ry thing can something do, but what kind of use are you?

Nay, nay little master, nay, do not serve me so, I pray,
Don't you see the wool that grows, on my back to make your clothes?
Cold, ah very cold you'd be, if you had not wool from me.

True, it seems a pleasant thing, nipping daisies in the spring,
But what chilly nights I pass, on the cold and dewy grass,
Or pick my scanty dinner where, all the ground is brown and bare.

Then the farmer comes at last, when the merry spring is past,
Cuts my woolly fleece away, for your coat in wintry day,
Little master, this is why, in the pleasant fields I lie.

For those of you who like a little learning with your songs!

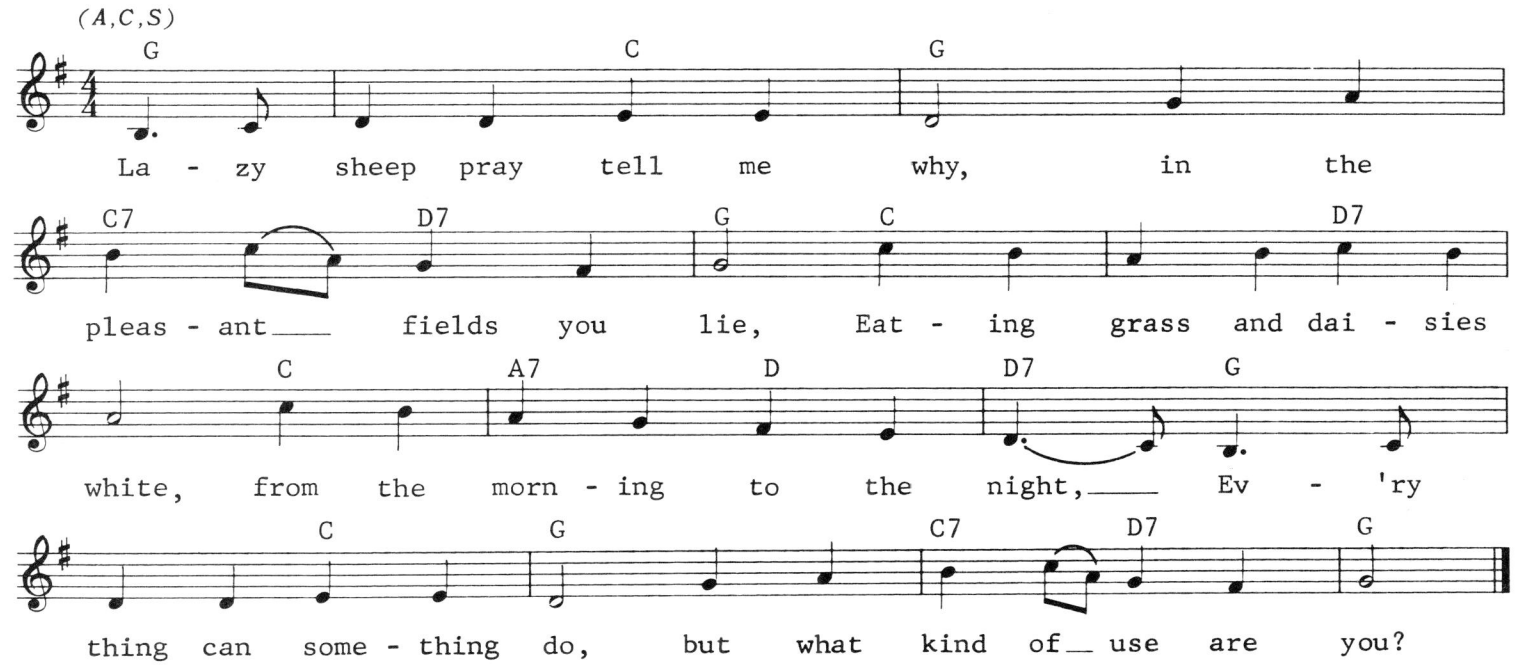

New River Train

Afro-American

Chorus:

```
      C
I'm ridin' on that new river train,

                              G⁷
I'm ridin' on that new river train,

C               F
Same o'le train that brought me here,

      G⁷        C
Gonna carry me back again.
```

Honey ya can't love one,
Honey ya can't love one,
Can't love one and still have fun,
Honey ya can't love one.

Two . . . and still be true.	Three . . . and still love me.
Four . . . and still love more.	Five . . . and stay alive.
Six . . . and still have kicks.	Seven . . . and go to heaven.
Eight . . . and still be great.	Nine . . . and still be mine.

Ten . . . so I'll say it again.

You must love all . . . both short and tall!

Chorus:
I'm ridin', etc.

A fun variation for the small children is for them to play "train" and shuffle around the room speeding up and slowing down—slowing both song and train as the leader sees fit.

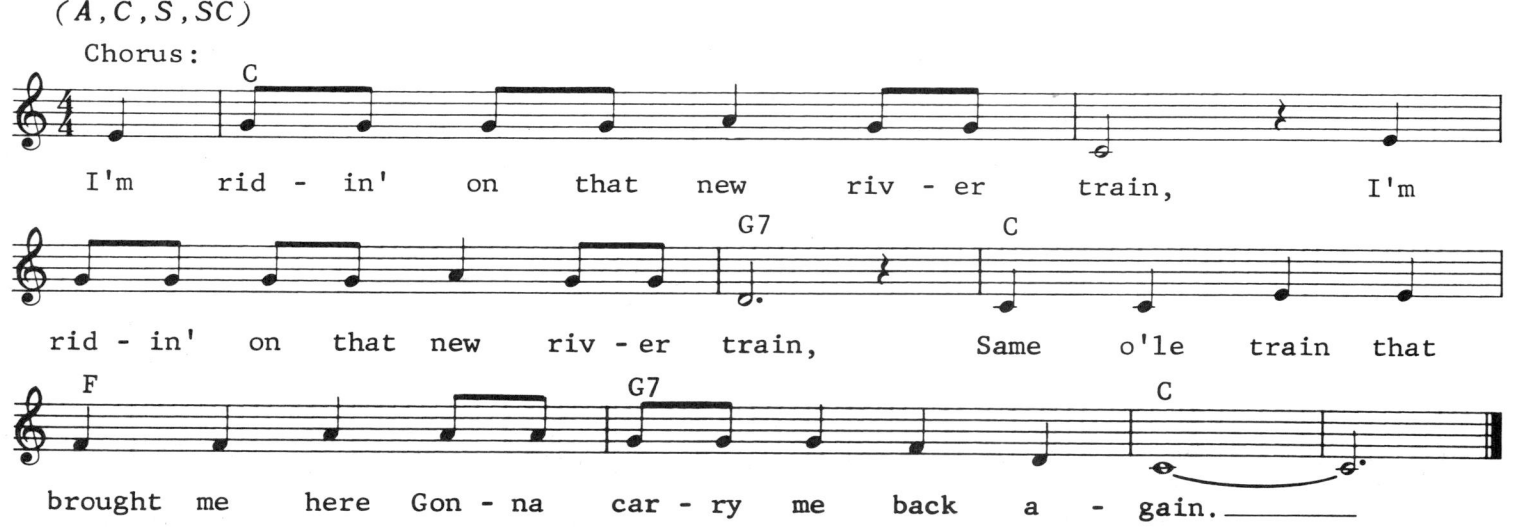

82

My Twenty Pennies

Venezuelan

         C
With twenty pennies, with twenty pennies, with twenty pennies,

 F   C
I bought a pava, (turkey)

   F   C   G⁷   C
The pava had a pavito, I have the pava and the pavito,

      G⁷   C
And thus I have yet my twenty pennies.

With twenty pennies, with twenty pennies, with twenty pennies,
I bought a gata, (cat)
The gata had a gatito, I have the gata and the gatito,
I have the pava and the pavito,
And thus I have yet my twenty pennies.

chiva	goat	**chivito**	baby goat	**lora**	parrot	**lorito**	baby parrot
mona	monkey	**monito**	baby monkey	**vaca**	cow	**vaquito**	baby cow

Spanish:
Con real y medio, con real y medio, con real y medio,
Compre una pava,
La pava tuvo un pavito, tengo la pava, tengo el pavito,
Y siempre me queda mi real y medio.

Here is an opportunity to learn a little Spanish as well as to test one's memory since as each animal is added, they must *all* be mentioned in each verse, only sung in reverse order on the line "I have the vaca and the vaquito, I have the lora and the lorito...etc." in Verse 6 for instance.

83

Risselty Rosselty

North American

G   C G
I married my wife in the month of June,

D⁷   G
Risselty Rosselty now, now, now!

G   C G
I carried her off by the light of the moon,

D⁷   G
Risselty Rosselty now, now, now!

Chorus:

G D⁷ G
Risselty Rosselty, Hey bombosity,

       D⁷
Nickety, nackety, reticule quality,

G D⁷ G
Willowby, wallowby now, now, now!

She swept the floor but once a year, Risselty, etc.
She swore her broom was much too dear, etc.

She combed her hair but once a year, etc.
With every rake she gave a tear, etc.

She churned the butter in Dad's old boot, etc.
And for a dasher she used her foot, etc.

The butter came out a grizzly grey, etc.
The cheese took legs and ran away,

The cheese and molasses are on the shelf, etc.
If you want some more verses you
  sing 'em yourself, etc.

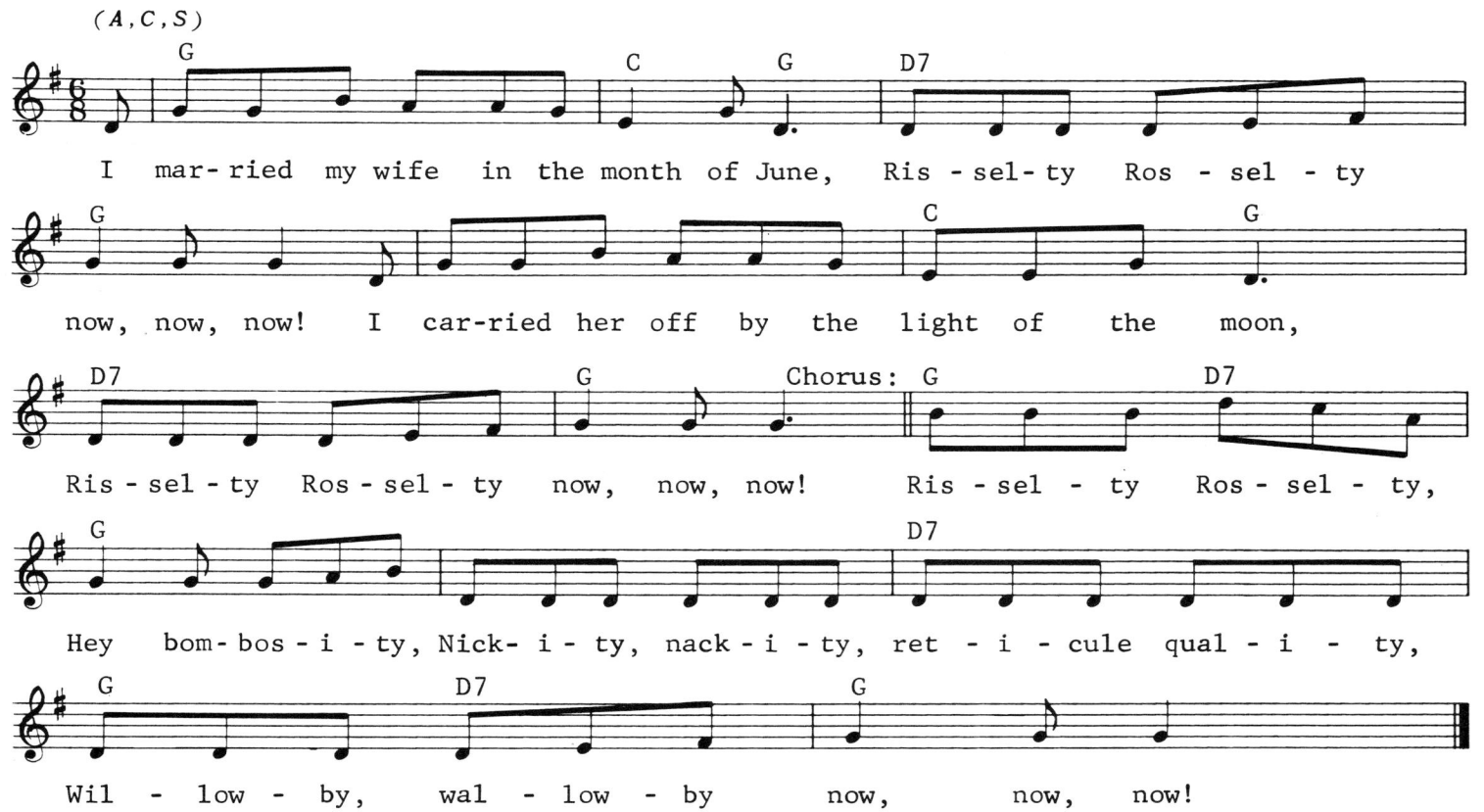

Who Did?

Afro-American

Leader	Children	All
E		
Who did,	Who did,	
Who did,	Who did,	Who did swallow Jo-Jo-Jo-Jo?

} 3x

A⁶ B⁷	A B⁷	A B⁷ E
Who did swallow Jonah,	Who did swallow Jonah?	Who did swallow Jonah down?

Whale did, etc.	Daniel, etc.	Gabriel, etc.
Whale did swallow Jo-Jo-Jo-Jo,	Daniel in the li-li-li-li,	Gabriel blow your trump-trump-trump-trump,
Whale did swallow Jonah up.	Daniel in the lion's den.	Gabriel blow your trumpet loud.

This is a response song and therefore lends itself wonderfully to a songleader and a group of children answering each other back and forth and finally all joining together for the last statement.

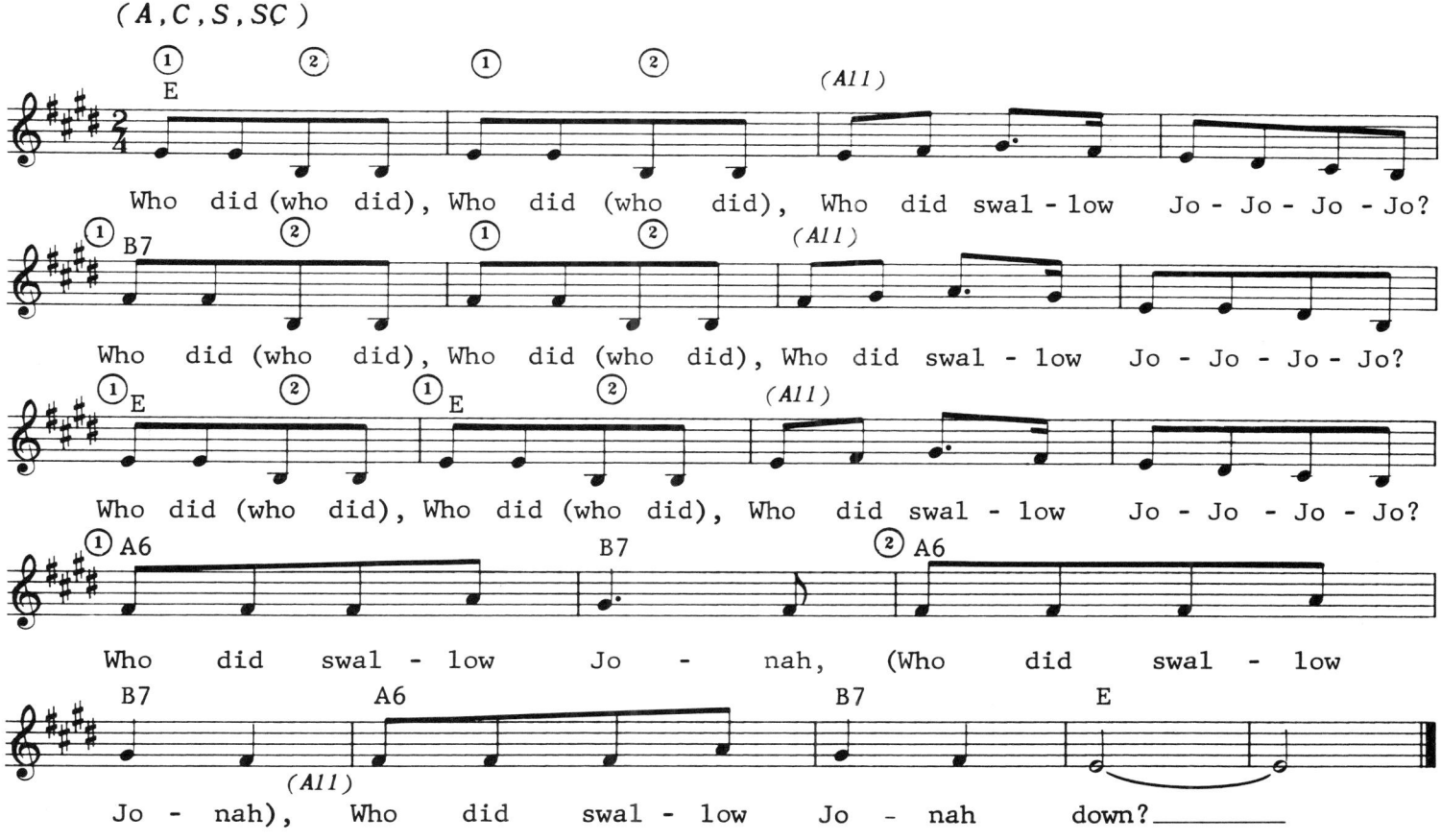

Almost Day (It's Almost Day)

Huddie Ledbetter

```
E                                   A     B⁷
Chickens crowin' from midnight, it's almost day,

                                   E B⁷   D
Chickens crowin' from midnight, it's almost day.
```

Santa Claus is comin', etc.

Candy canes & sugar plums, etc.

We're peepin' 'round the corner, etc.

Hang your stockings on the chimney, for Christmas Day, (2x)

I want a size 40 stocking, on Christmas Day, etc.

Santa Claus is comin', it's almost day, etc.

Chicken's crowin' from midnight, it's almost day, etc.

Since this is a holiday song, it can be done with a simple harmony line added for a selected chorus to sing.

Pat-A-Pan

French Traditional Carol

             Dm   Gm   Dm   A⁷

Now we'll play upon the drum and we'll make our voices hum,

                       Dm   A⁷

We'll be joyous as we play, Tu-re-lu-re-lu, Pat-a-pat-a-pan,

                     Dm   Gm A⁷   Dm

We'll be joyous as we play on a Merry Christmas Day.

Just as men of other days raised their voices loud in praise, etc.

Brotherhood will rule and then peace on earth will come to men, etc.

(A,C,S,SC)

Now we'll play up-on the drum and we'll make our voic-es hum, We'll be joy-ous as we play, Tu-re-lu-re-lu, Pat-a-pat-a-pan, We'll be joy-ous as we play on a Mer-ry Christ-mas Day.

Oh, In The Woods

English

Leader	Children
G   C
Oh in the woods,	Oh, in the woods,
There was a tree,	There was a tree,
The cutest little tree,	The cutest little tree,
D⁷
That I ever did see,	That I ever did see.

All

  G
The tree was in the hole,

And the hole in the ground,

                   G   C
And the green grass grew around, all around,

    G   D⁷   G
And the green grass grew all around.

Leader	*Children*
And on that tree,	And on that tree,
There was a limb,	There was a limb,
The cutest little limb,	The cutest little limb,
That I ever did see.	That I ever did see,

All

The limb was on the tree,
And the tree was in the hole,
And the hole was in the ground,
And the green grass grew all around, all around,
And the green grass grew all around.

And on that limb, . . . there was a branch, etc.

And on that branch, . . . there was a nest, etc.

And in that nest, . . . there was an egg, etc.

And in that egg, . . . there was a bird, etc.

And on that bird, . . . there was a wing, etc.

And on that wing, . . . there was a bug, etc.

And on that bug, . . . there was an eyelash, etc.

And on that eyelash . . . there was a germ, etc.

This song, too, can go on for as long as the children can keep adding more things to go on the germ (bacteria?) and because it is a response song, it makes for immediate total involvement of everyone in earshot!

(A,C,)

(Leader)   (Children)

Oh, in the woods, (Oh, in the woods) There was a tree, (There

was a tree) The cut-est lit-tle tree, (The cut-est lit-tle tree) That I

ev-er did see, (That I ev-er did see). The tree was in a hole and the

hole was in the ground, And the green grass grew all a-

- round, all a-round, and the green grass grew all a-round.

Let Us Come In (Party Crasher's Carol)

Malvina Reynolds

E
We are three wand'ring trav'lers,

               B⁷
Out in the wind and the rain.

We saw your light, cheery and bright,

                E
And tapped at your window pane, singing,

Refrain:

C#m
Let us come in,

E   G#m   B⁷
Let us come in, into your house so gay,

F#m
Let us come in,

B⁷
Let us come in,

               E
Please do not send us away.

We heard the music playing,
We smelled the beautiful stews,
One of us said, "Let's knock on the door!"
The other said, "What can we lose?" singing:

Please go ahead with your dinner,
We will just wait till you're through,
But if you find there's enough to go round,
Save us a beefsteak or two, singing:

One or two extra won't matter,
Plenty of room on the floor,
You'll look around and find we have gone
After a fortnight or more, singing:

One of us plays on the whistle,
Makes such a musical tweet,
One of us sings such beautiful things,
And one keeps time with his feet, singing:

We will make noise very softly,
The landlord won't hear us at all,
And if there's not enough room in the beds,
We will just sleep in the hall, singing:

We are three wan - d'ring trav - 'lers,_____ Out in the

wind and the rain._____ We saw your light, cheer - y and

bright, And tapped at your win - dow pane,_____ sing - ing,

Refrain:

Let us come in, Let us come in, in - to your

house so gay,_____ Let us come in, Let us come

in, Please do not send us a - way._____

No House

Malvina Reynolds

```
       F                   Em
Oh the cat has a house, and the rat has a house,

       Dm                      C    C⁷
And the dog and the mouse and the flea;

       F                Em         Am
And the snail has a house and the whale has a house,

       Dm      G⁷        C
And they all have a house but me.
```

```
     F         Em           Dm         C     C⁷
The sign on ev'ry building says, "No children wanted here."

      F         C      A⁷    D⁷          G⁷
When I grow up the sign will say: "Landlords kindly stay away."

      F                  Em
Oh the cow has a house and the sow has a house,

       Dm                       G⁷
And the Pentagon takes lots of scenery;
```

```
       C                    G⁷
There's hangars for planes, roundhouses for trains,

C                  Dm
Garages for cars and taverns for bars,

Em                 F
Buildings for stores with seventeen floors,

    G      Em     Am       D⁷
And money enough for three world wars,

       Dm        G⁷       C
But they couldn't build a house for me.
```

Lullabies and Sleepytime Songs.

"Hush Little Baby"

Eventually, everyone needs a rest from whatever they're doing, no matter how much they may love what they're doing. Little children usually have to be persuaded (even some adults, also) and one of the easiest and most enjoyable ways, whether it be beddy-bye time at home or rest-time at school, is through a lullaby. The most energetic child will rest a few minutes while listening, lolling, and being lulled into the fantasy world of some of the following beautiful songs.

Go To Sleepy Little Baby

North American

```
G              C   G              C
Go to sleepy little baby, go to sleepy little baby,

G                    C                    G         D⁷ G
When you wake we'll patty - patty cake and ride a tiny little pony.
```

(A,C,S)

Go to sleep - y lit - tle ba - by, go to

sleep - y lit - tle ba - by, When you wake we'll

pat - ty - pat - ty - cake and ride a ti - ny lit - tle po - ny.

Sleep, Baby, Sleep

North American

CFC F CFC G⁷   CFC   G⁷ CFC G⁷
Sleep, baby sleep, close your eyes and go to sleep.

CFC F   CFC G⁷   CFC   G⁷ CFC
Rest, baby rest, close your eyes and softly rest.

G⁷   CFC   G⁷   CFC
Oh your daddy he's gone away,

G⁷   CFC   G⁷   CFC G⁷
And your mommy, she's here to stay, so:

Back to beginning

C   F   C   F
Loo, loo, loo, loo, etc. (2x)

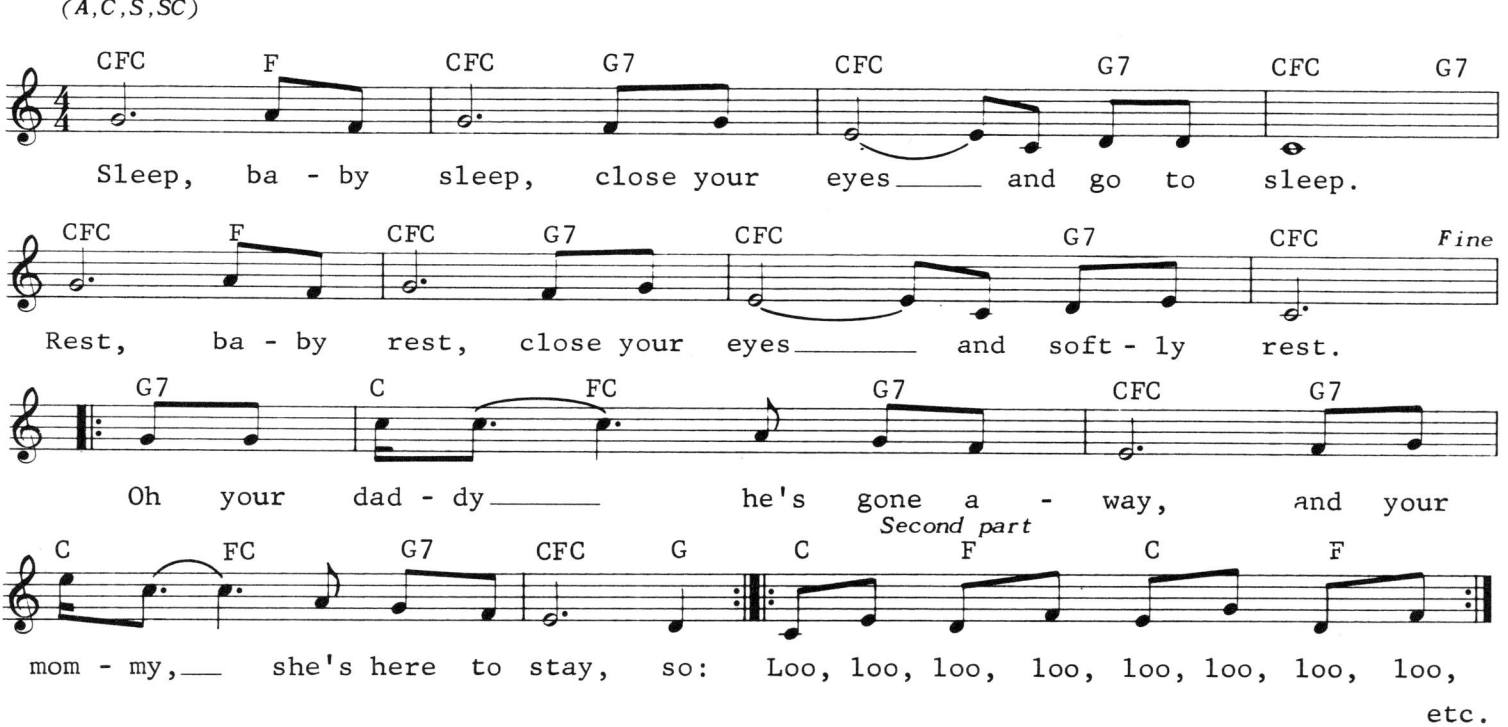

Children sing the song through once in unison. Then while half the group continues repeating the
"Loo, los" second part over and over again, the other half sings the song again.

Cradle Song

Franz Schubert

D   A⁷   D   A⁷
Slumber, slumber, sweet my joy and treasure,

D   A⁷   D   A⁷   D
Gently, gently, rocked by mother's hand.

A⁷   D   G A⁷
Golden slumbers, dreams of azure,

D   A⁷   D   A⁷   D
Hover 'round thee safe in slumberland.

Slumber, slumber, in thy nest enfolding,
Slumber, sheltered by thy mother's arm.
All her treasure, bright and golden,
Mother's love now keep thee safe from harm.

Slumber, slumber, till thine eyes unclosing,
"Loo-la, loo-la," mother's voice will sing.
Two white lilies, two red roses,
When thou wakest she her babe will bring.

Hush Little Baby

North American

```
G                          D⁷
Hush little baby don't say a word,

                           G
Mama's gonna buy you a mockin'-bird.

G                          D⁷
If that mockin'-bird don't sing,

                              G
Papa's gonna buy you a diamond ring.
```

If that ring is made of brass,
Mama's gonna buy you a lookin' glass.

If that lookin' glass gets broke,
Papa's gonna buy you a billy goat.

If that billy goat don't pull,
Mama's gonna buy you a cart and bull.

If that cart and bull turn over,
Papa's gonna buy you a dog named Rover.

If that dog named Rover don't bark,
Mama's gonna buy you a horse and cart.

If that horse and cart fall down,
You'll be the sweetest little boy in town!

2nd Version:

Hush little baby, don't you fret,
Daddy's gonna buy you a super-jet.

If the super-jet won't fly,
You'll get a rocket by and by.

If the rocket doesn't lift,
Daddy's gonna buy you another gift.

Daddy's gonna buy you a satellite,
To take you into lunar flight.

If the satellite won't go 'round,
Daddy's gonna take you back to the ground.

Hush little baby, don't you frown,
You'll be the cutest space-cadet in town.

3rd Version:

Hush little baby, don't you complain,
Mama's gonna buy you an air-o-plane.

If the air-o-plane won't fly,
Mama's gonna buy you some apple pie.

If the apple's no good,
Mama's gonna get a nice warm hood.

If that nice warm hood won't wear,
Mama's gonna buy you a black toy bear.

If that bear won't talk,
Mama's gonna buy you a box of chalk.

If the chalk won't write,
Mama's gonna buy you a big red kite.

If the kite comes down,
You'll still be the most complainin' baby in town!

(A,C,S)

1. Hush, lit-tle ba - by don't say a word, Ma - ma's gon - na buy you a

mock - in' bird. If that mock - in' bird don't sing,

Pa - pa's gon - na buy you a dia - mond ring. ba - by in town!

There Were Ten In The Bed!

North American

```
                E        A    E
There were ten in the bed and the little one said:

         A    E    A
"Roll over, roll over!"

               A   E      A   E
So they all rolled over and one fell out.
```

There were nine in the bed and the little one said, etc.

There were eight in the, etc.

There were seven in the, etc.

There were six in the, etc.

There were five in the, etc.

There were four in the, etc.

There were three in the, etc.

There were two in the, etc.

There was one in the bed and the little one said: "GOOD NIGHT!" *Shouted!*

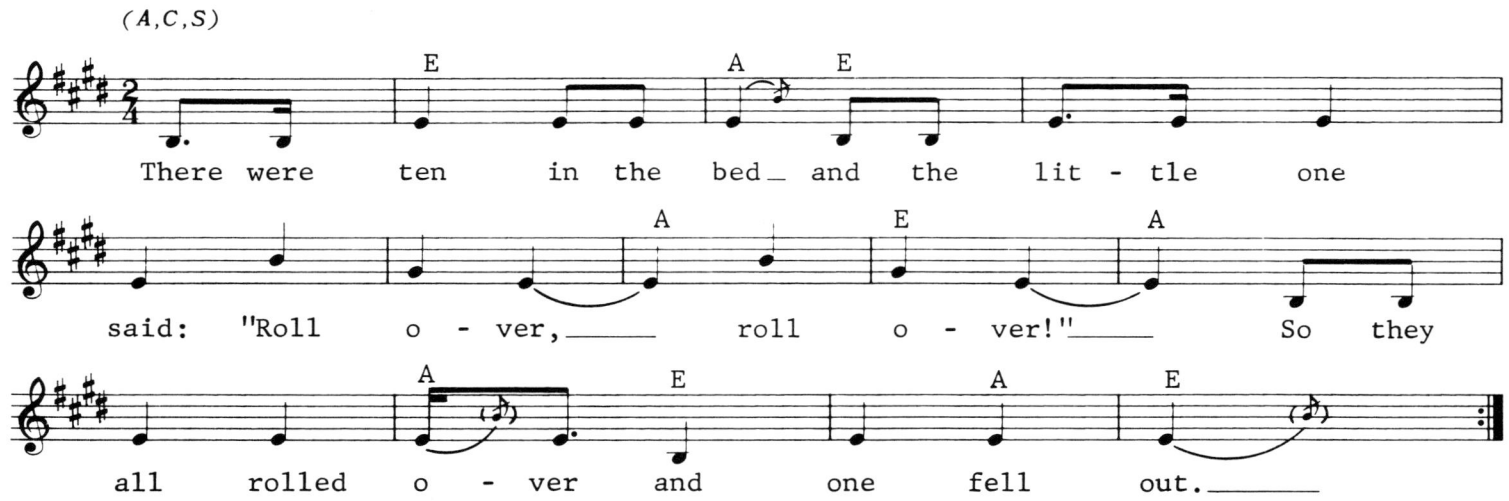

All The Pretty Little Horses

North American

```
Em              Am              B⁷              Em
Hush-a-buy, don't you cry, go to sleepy little baby.

Em              Am              Bm⁷            Em
When you wake, you shall have, all the pretty little horses.


Refrain:

Em              Am              Bm⁷                    Em
Black and bays, dapples and grays, all the pretty little horses.


Way down yonder in the meadow, lies a poor little lambie,
Bees and butterflies pickin' on it's eyes, poor little thing is cryin' "Mammy."

Hum....
When you wake, you shall have, all the pretty little horses.
```

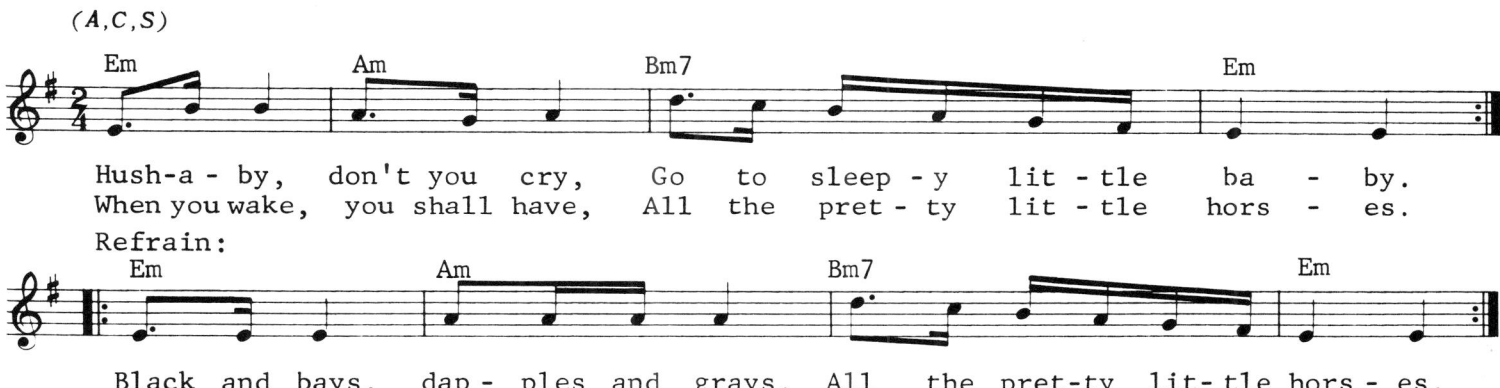

Children's Prayer

(from Hansel and Gretel)
Englebert Humperdinck

A   D A   E⁷
When at night I go to sleep, fourteen angels watch do keep,

Bm A   E⁷ Bm
Two my head are guarding, two my feet are guiding,

G⁷ C A⁷ A⁷   E A
Two are on my right hand and two are on my left hand,

D   A A⁷   Em D
Two who o'er me hover, two above to cover,

     Bm B⁷   E⁷ A
Two to me are given to guide my steps to heaven!

Go Tell Aunt Rhody

Traditional

D(Dm)   A⁷   D(Dm)
Go tell Aunt Rhody, go tell Aunt Rhody,

                         G(Gm) A⁷   D(Dm)
Go tell Aunt Rhody the old grey goose is dead.

The one she was saving (3x)
To make a feather bed.

She died in the mill-pond (3x)
Standing on her head.

The goslings are crying (3x)
Because their mother's dead.

The gander is mourning (3x)
Because his wife is dead.

An interesting variation on this song is to treat Verse I as a chorus and sing it in the major key, singing the remaining verses in the minor key and returning to the "major chorus" after each of the other verses.

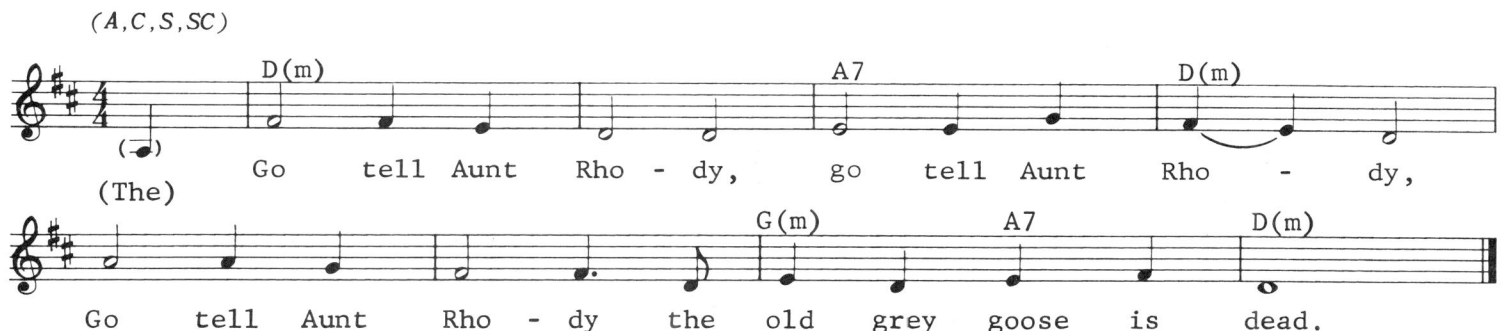

All Through The Night

Welsh

```
G        C       A      D       C D⁷      G
Sleep, my child, let peace attend thee, all through the night,

G        C       A      D      C D⁷       G
Guardian angels God will send thee, all through the night;

C                                  Am⁶            D⁷
Soft the drowsy hours are creeping, hill and vale in slumber steeping,

G   C    A    D     C D⁷     G
I, my loving vigil keeping, all through the night.
```

While the moon her watch is keeping, all through the night,
While the weary world is sleeping, all through the night;
O'er thy spirit gently stealing, visions of delight revealing,
Breathes a pure and holy feeling, all through the night.

Deep the silence 'round us spreading, all through the night,
Dark the path that we are treading, all through the night;
Though our hearts be wrapt in sorrow, from the hope of dawn we borrow,
Promise of a glad tomorrow, all through the night.

Now The Day Is Over

Joseph Barnby (1868) and Sabine Baring-Gould

C   G⁷   C   Am   E⁷   Am
Now the day is over, night is drawing nigh,

F   D⁷   C   G   G⁷   C
Shadows of the evening, steal across the sky.

Grant to all the weary, calm and sweet repose,
With the tendrest blessing, may our eyelids close.

Grant to little children, all that they might see,
Guard the sailors' tossing, on the deep. blue sea.

When the morning wakens, then may I arise,
Pure and fresh and hopeful, sunrise in my eyes.

Lullabye For Heidi

Ruth C. Cohn

(To those children who at times fear the night. R.C.C.)

     E
My child, when we turn off the light,

    B⁷
And when we kiss each other good night,

     A   E
Think of the stars that always shine,

    B⁷   E
And moon and heaven they all are thine.

Your own are wind and flowers and trees,
And lightening bugs and bumble-bees,
Your cover hugs you warm and tight,
God lives in darkness as in light.

My darling, 'til the curtains rise,
The stars will shine within your eyes,
They sparkle golden all the night,
Sleep well my child in your inner light.

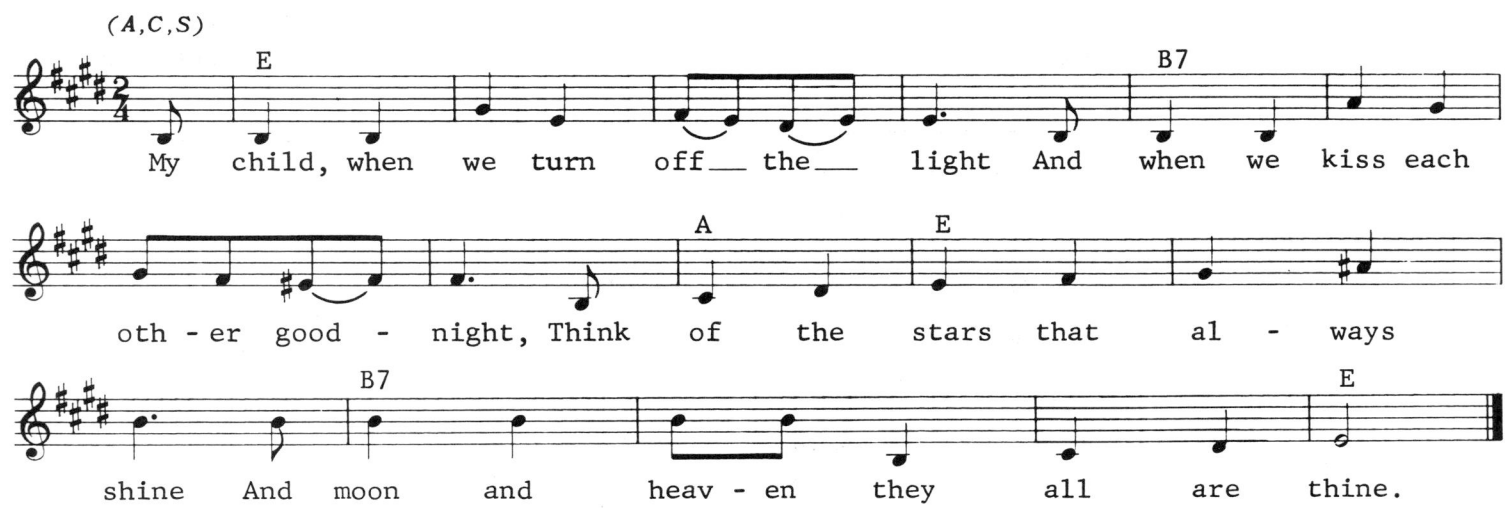

This simple and beautiful lullaby was taught to me by Ruth Cohn, who wrote it for her daughter Heidi around 1949.

Mommy's Girl

Malvina Reynolds

Chorus:

C
This is the girl that Mommy loves,

G⁷   C
This is the girl that Mommy loves,

F   C
This is the girl that Mommy loves,

G⁷   C
Sweetest girl in town.

F
Up in the morning break of day,

C
Into her clothes and out to play,

G⁷
Breakfast somewhere along the way,

          C
Bouncing up and down.

Now she's an engine, clear the track,
Now she's a hammer and smacks a tack,
Now she's a sack on a piggy back,
Fifty cents a pound.

Now she's a daddy and works in a store,
Now she's a mommy and sweeps the floor,
Now she's a girl in a pinafore,
Ruffles all around.

Stars are out and it's time for bed,
Here's the pajamas white and red,
Here's the pillow for sleepy head,
Lay the beany down.

107

Turn Around

Malvina Reynolds, Alan Greene, and Harry Belafonte

```
C            Em        F        G⁷
Where are you going my little one, little one,
```

```
C            Em        G⁷       G
Where are you going my baby, my own?
```

```
      C           C⁷      F              Fm
Turn around and you're two, turn around and you're four,
```

```
      C           Em           G⁷        C
Turn around and you're a young girl going out of my door.
```

Chorus:
```
          C
Turn around, turn around,
```

```
      F           Em           G⁷       C
Turn around and you're a young girl going out of my door.
```

Where are you going, my little one, little one,
Little dirndls and petticoats, where have you gone,
Turn around and you're tiny, turn around and you're grown,
Turn around and you're a young wife with babes of your own.

108

One Grain Of Sand

Pete Seeger

Dm
One grain of sand,

G   F
One grain of sand in all the world,

Dm
One grain of sand,

G   Am   Dm
One little boy, one little girl.

One grain of sand, one little star up in the sky,
One grain of sand, one little you, one little I.

One grain of sand, one drop of wa-ter in the sea,
One grain of sand, one little you, one little me.

One grain of sand, one leaf of grass on a windy plain,
One grain of sand, we come and go again and again,
    again, and again, again and again.

I love you so, I love you so, I love you so, I love you so,
More than you will ever, ever, ever, ever know.

One grain of sand, one little snowflake lost in the swirling storm,
One grain of sand, I'll hold you close and keep you warm.

One grain of sand, one grain of sand on an endless shore,
One grain of sand, one little life, who'd ask for more?

One grain of sand, one grain of sand, one grain of sand,
One grain of sand, one grain of sand, one grain of sand.

M-m-m-m-m-m, one little star, up in the blue,
M-m-m-m-m-m, one little me, one little you.

Brown Baby

Oscar Brown, Jr.

```
      Dm                  Gm
Brown Baby, Brown Baby, as you grow up,

 Dm                   Gm     A⁷
I want you to drink from the plenty cup;

 Dm        F       Dm
I want you to stand up tall and proud,

 Gm        Dm       A
I want you to speak up clear and loud;

      A  Dm
Brown Baby.
```

Brown Baby, Brown Baby, as years roll by,
I want you to go with your head held high;
I want you to love by the justice code,
I want you to walk down by the freedom road;
Brown Baby.

```
     Gm             Dm
Now lie away, lie away sleeping,

Gm              Dm
Lie away here in my arms;

        Gm                  Dm
While your daddy and mommy protect you

     F              Gm
And keep you safe from harm;

     Gm⁶
Oh, you little Brown Baby.
```

Brown Baby, Brown Baby, it makes me glad,
That you will have things I never had;
When out of men's hearts all the hate is hurled,
You're gonna live in a better world;
Brown Baby.

Brown__ Ba - by, Brown Ba - by, as you grow__ up, I want you to drink from the plen - ty cup; I want you to stand up tall and__ proud, I want you to speak up clear and loud; Brown__ Ba - by.__ Brown__ Now lie a - way, lie a - way, sleep - ing,__ Lie a - way here in my arms __ While your dad - dy and mom - my pro - tect you __ __ And keep you__ safe__ from harm; Oh, you lit - tle Brown__

Fine

D.S. al Fine

Liverpool Lullaby

Words and Music by Stan Kelly

Dm   A   A⁷   Dm
Ah you are a mucky kid, dirty as a dust-bin lid,

Dm   A   Gm   Dm   A⁷   Dm
When he finds out the things you did, you'll get a belt from your dad.

Gm   Dm   A   Dm
And you have your father's nose, so crimson in the dark it glows,

Gm   Dm   A⁷   Dm
If you're not asleep when the boozer's close, you'll get a belt from your dad.

You look so scruffy lyin' there, strawberry jam tops in your hair,
And in the world you haven't a care, and I have got so many.
It's quite a struggle every day, livin' on your father's pay,
The bugger drinks it all away and leaves me without any.

Although we have no silver spoon, better days are comin' soon,
Now Nellie's workin' at the loom, and she gets paid on Friday.
Perhaps some day we'll have a bash, when Littlewoods provide the cash,
We'll get a house in Knotty Ash, and buy your dad a brewery.

Ah you are a mucky kid, dirty as a dust-bin lid,
When he finds out the things you did, you'll get a belt from your dad
Ah you have your father's face, you're growin' up a real hard case,
But there's no one else can take your place, go fast asleep for mummy.

October Winds

Adapted by Pat Clancy, Tom Clancy, Liam Clancy and Tommy Makem

     C   F   C   F   C
The October winds lament around the Castle of Dromore,

     Am   G   C   F   G⁷   C
Yet peace is in her lofty halls, my loving treasure store;

            F   C   G⁷   C
Though autumn leaves may droop and die, a bud of Spring are you,

     Dm   C Am   Dm   G⁷   C
Sing hush-a-by loo, la-loo lo-lan, sing hush-a-by loo-la low.

Bring no ill-will to hinder us, my helpless babe and me,
Dread spirits of the Blackwater, Clan Owen's wild banshee;
And holy voices granting us whatever be our due,
Sing hush-a-by loo, la-loo lo-lan, sing hush-a-by loo-la low.

Take time to thrive my ray of hope in the garden of Dromore,
Take heed young eaglet till thy wings are feathered fit to soar;
A little rest and then the world is full of work to do,
Sing hush-a-by loo, la-loo lo-lan, sing hush-a-by loo-la low.

O Can Ye Sew Cushions

Scottish

```
    C
O can ye sew cushions and can ye sew sheets?

                     G⁷          C
And can ye sing Ba-la-loo when the bairn greets?

   D⁷       C        D⁷       Am
So hee and bawbirdie and hee and bawlamb,

    C        G⁷           C
And hee and bawbirdie my bonnie wee doo.
```

Chorus:
```
C              G⁷        C
Hee oh wee oh, what will I do wi' you,

              G⁷    C
Black's the life I lead wi' you,

            G⁷    C
Mony o' you, little for t'gie you,

                   G⁷    C
Hee oh wee oh, what will I do wi' you?
```

Now hush a-baw lammie, and hush a-baw dear,
Now hush a-baw lammie, thy minnie is here,
The wild wind is ravin' thy minnie's heart's sair,
The wild wind is ravin' but ye dinna care.

Sing ballaloo lammie, sing ballaloo dear,
Does wee lammie ken that its daddie's no here?
Ye're rockin' fu' sweetly on mammie's warm knee,
But daddie's a rockin' upon the saut sea.

I biggit the cradle on the tree top,
And the wind it did blaw, and the cradle did rock,
And hee and baw birdie, and hee and baw lamb,
And hee and baw birdie, my bonnie wee doo.

mony	many
t'gie	to give
minnie	mama
sair	sore
biggit	built

(A,C,S,SC)

Oh can ye sew cush-ions and can ye sew sheets? And can ye sing__ Ba-la-loo__ when the bairn greets? So hee and baw- bird-ie and hee and baw- lamb, And hee and baw- bird-ie my bon-nie wee doo.

Chorus:

Hee oh wee oh, what will I do wi' you, Black's the life I lead wi'__ you, Mo-ny o' you, lit-tle for t'-gie you, Hee oh wee oh, what will I do_____ wi' you?

115

A Las Puertas Del Cielo
(At The Gates Of Heaven)

Spanish-American
English and Descant: A. D. Zanzig

F   C⁷   F   C⁷
A las puertas del cielo venden zapatos,

F   G⁷ F   G⁷
Para los angelitos que andan descalzos,

F   B♭ C⁷ F   C⁷   F   C⁷ F   C⁷F
Duermete niño, duermete niño, duermete niño, aroo, aroo.

A los niños que duermen Dios los bendice,
A las madres que velan Dios los asiste,
Duermete niño, duermete niño, duermete, niño, aroo, aroo.

English:

F   C⁷   F
At the gates little shoes they are selling,

F   C⁷   F   C⁷
For the bare-footed angels dwelling,

F   B♭⁷ F   C⁷   F   C⁷ F   C⁷C
Slumber my baby, slumber my baby, slumber my baby, aroo, aroo.

God will bless the children so peacefully sleeping,
God will help the mothers whose love they are keeping,
Slumber my baby, slumber my baby, slumber my baby, aroo, aroo.

Descant:
At the gates little shoes they are selling, etc.
God will bless so peacefully sleeping, etc.

When I did this with a selected chorus I had them sing it through once in Spanish and then in English when I had about 10 voices on the Descant.

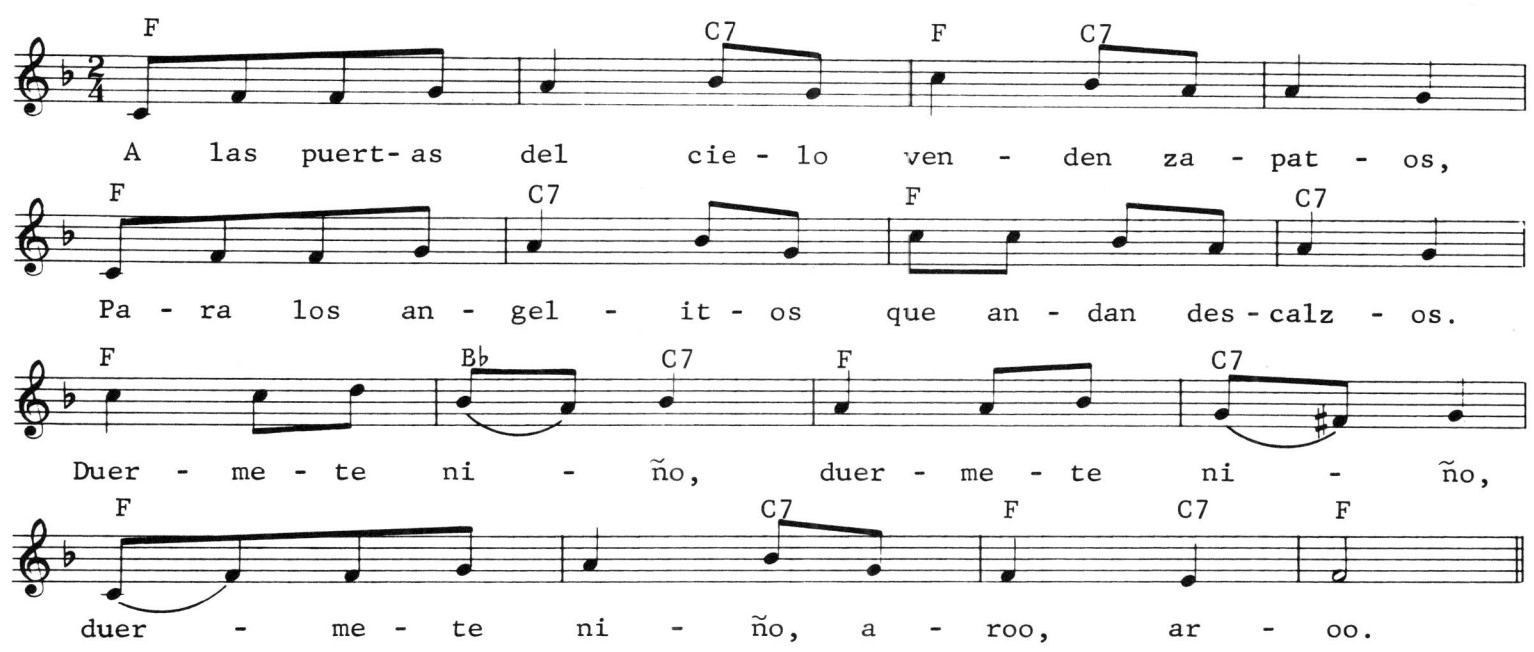

A las puert-as del cie - lo ven - den za - pat - os,

Pa - ra los an - gel - it - os que an - dan des - calz - os.

Duer - me - te ni - ño, duer - me - te ni - ño,

duer - me - te ni - ño, a - roo, ar - oo.

Descant

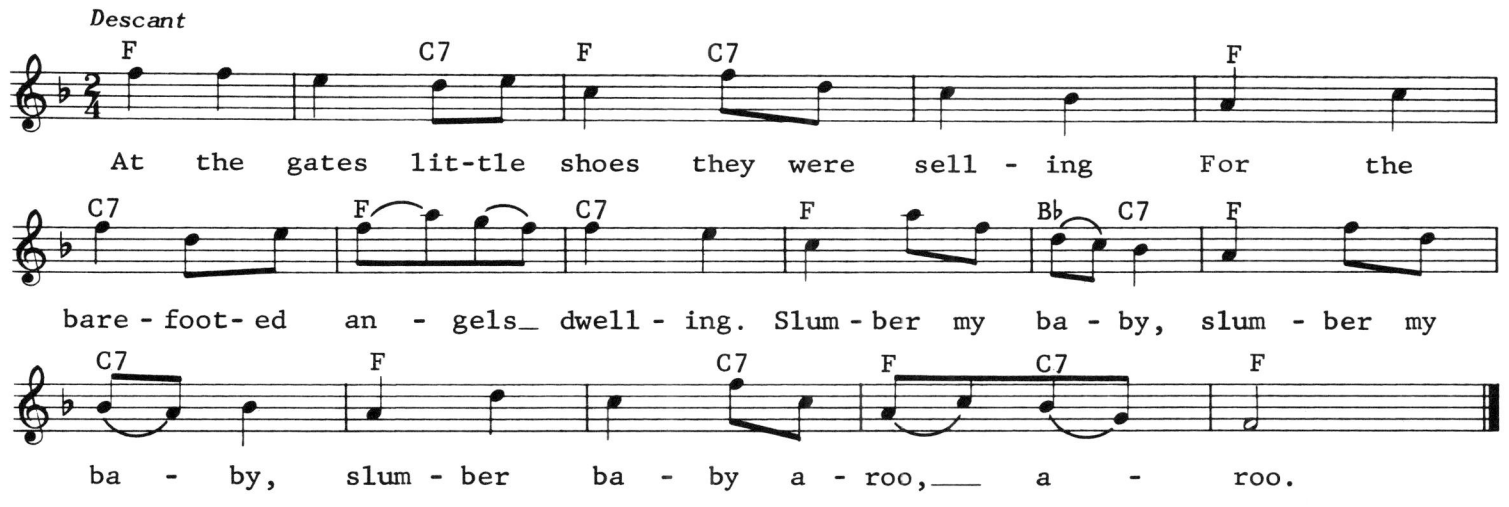

At the gates lit-tle shoes they were sell - ing For the

bare - foot - ed an - gels_ dwell - ing. Slum - ber my ba - by, slum - ber my

ba - by, slum - ber ba - by a - roo,___ a - roo.

El Coquí (The Tree Frog)

Puerto Rican
English: Olcutt Saunders

  A   D   A   E⁷   A

A El coquí, el co**D**quí a mi me en**A**canta, es tan lindo **E⁷**el cantar del co**A**quí;

Por las no**D**ches al ir a a**A**costarme, me a**E⁷**dormece cantando a**A**sí:

E⁷Co-quí! **A**Co-quí! **E⁷**Co-quí-qií-quí-**A**quí!

E⁷Co-quí! **A**Co-quí! **E⁷**Co-quí-quí-quí-**A**quí!

English:
The coqui sings a lullaby softly,
I can hear the coqui all night long;
Though I fall fast asleep when it's bedtime,
In my dreams comes his sweet little song:
Co-kee! Co-kee! Co-kee-kee-kee-kee!
Co-kee! Co-kee! Co-kee-kee-kee-kee!

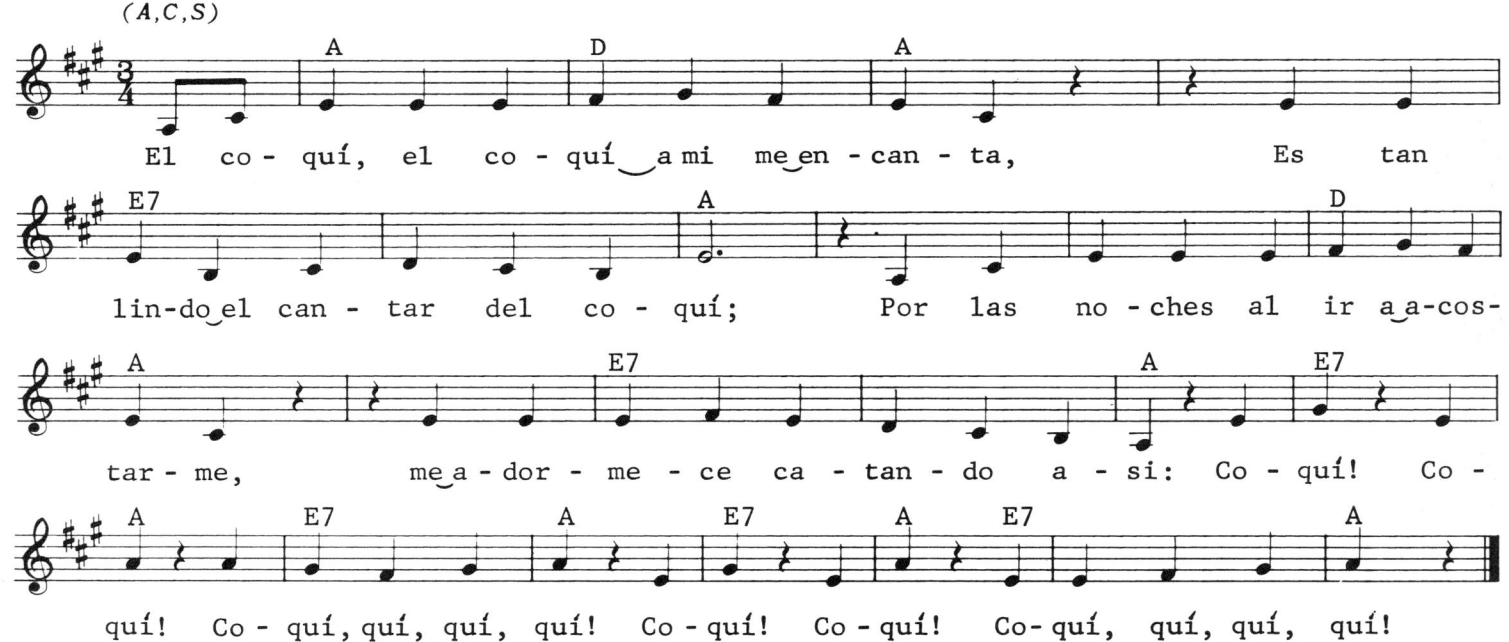

118

Coventry Carol

Old English
Robert Croo

Dm   A⁷Dm   Gm⁶   A
Lully, lullay, thou little tiny child,

Dm   Gm A⁷Dm
By, by, lully,   lullay,

    Gm   A⁷   Gm⁶ A⁷
Lullay, thou little tiny child,

D   Gm A⁷D
By, by, lully,   lullay.

O sisters too, how may we do,
For to preserve this day,
This poor youngling for whom we do sing,
By, by, lully, lullay?

Herod the king in his raging,
Charged he hath this day,
His men of might in his own sight,
All children young to slay.

Then woe is me, poor child for thee,
And never mourn and say,
For they parting nor say or sing,
By, by, lully, lullay.

Lully, lullay, thou little tiny child,
By, by, lullay,
For kings all die but baby live,
To sing on Christmas Day.

(A , C , S , SC , E)

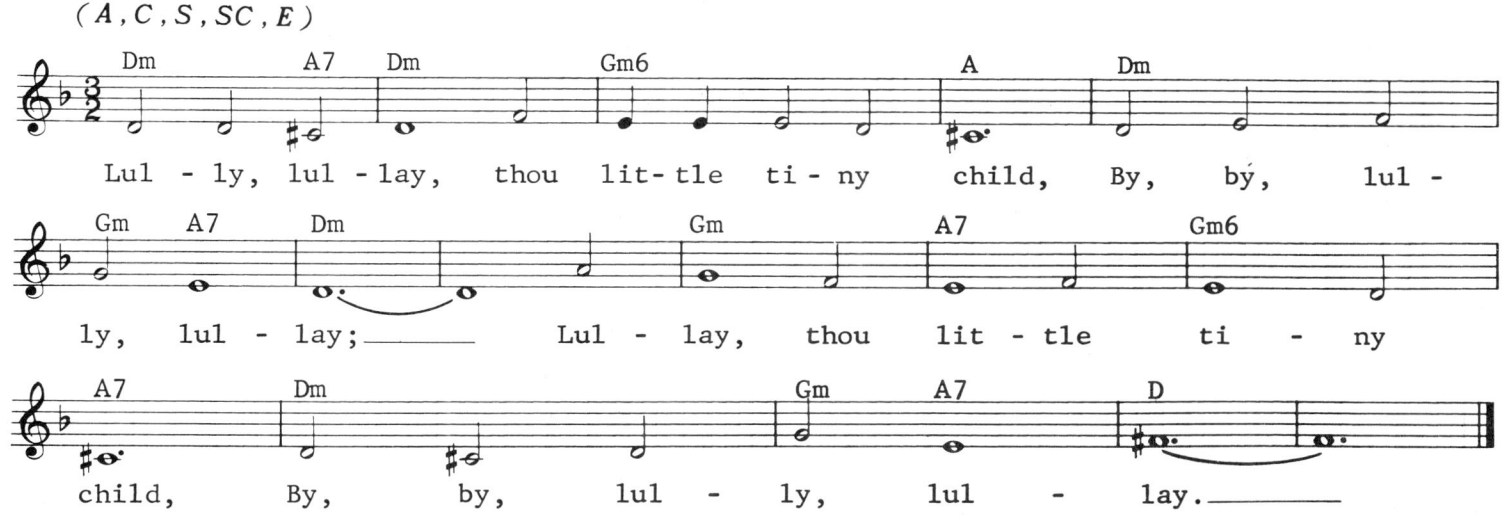

119

Sweet Potatoes

West Indian
Hector Spaulding

From *Twice 55—The New Brown Book;* copyright © 1929
by Summy-Birchard Company, Evanston, Illinois.
Copyright renewed. All rights reserved. Used by Permission.

B⁷   E   B⁷
Soon as we all cook sweet potatoes, sweet potatoes, sweet potatoes,

B⁷   E   B⁷   E
Soon as we all cook sweet potatoes, eat 'em right straight up!

Soon as supper's et, mommy hollers, mommy hollers, mommy hollers,
Soon as supper's et, mommy hollers, get along to bed.

Soon's we touch our heads to the pillow, etc.
. . . , go to sleep right smart.

Soon's the rooster crows in the mornin', etc.
. . . , gotta wash our face.

Soon's the school bus stops on the highway, etc.
. . . , got to go to school.

Soon's the last bell rings after school's out, etc.
. . . , got to get right home.

Harmony line:

B⁷   E   B⁷   E
Roo, roo, roo, roo, roo, roo, Sing holy dinkum!

B⁷   E   B⁷   E
Roo, roo, roo, roo, roo, roo, Roo, roo!

(A,C,S,SC)

Soon as we all cook sweet po - ta - toes,
Roo, roo, roo, roo, roo,

sweet po - ta - toes, sweet po - ta - toes, Soon as we all
roo, Sing ho - ly dink - um! Roo, roo, roo,

cook sweet po - ta - toes, eat 'em right straight up!
roo, roo, roo, Roo, roo!

Do Do (Sleep)

Haitian (Creole)

C F G⁷   C   F G⁷   C
Dodo ti titite manman'l, Dodo ti titite manman'l,

F   C   G⁷   C F   C   G⁷   C
Si li pa dodo crab-la va mange'l, si li pa dodo crab-la va mange'l.

Mama li pralé la riviĕ, Papa li pralé péché crab,

Si li pa dodo crab-la va mange'l, si li pa dodo crab-la va mange'l.

Coda:

C   G⁷ C   G⁷ C
Dodo titite crab la calalou, dodo titite crab la calalou.

English:
Sleep, sleep, mama's own little one, (2x)
    if you don't sleep, lobsters will eat you. (2x)

Your mother will go to the river, your daddy is going to fish,
    if you don't sleep, lobsters will eat you. (2x)

Coda:
Sleep, my own little one, lobsters will be your food. (2x)

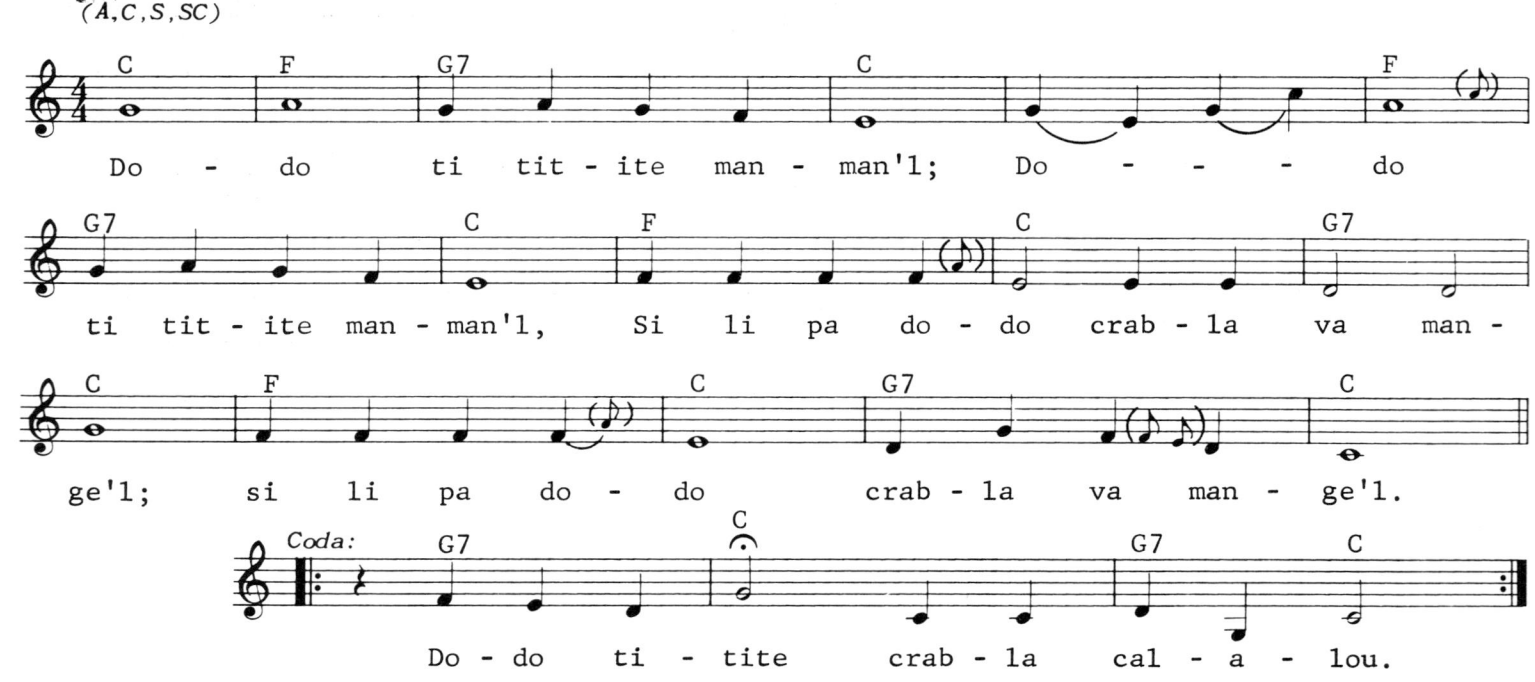

Rozenkes Mit Mandlen
(Raisins and Almonds)

Yiddish

      Dm
Unter yeedele vigele, shteyta klor tsigele,

   A⁷   Dm   Gm   Dm
Dos tsigele is geforen handlen, dos vet zine dine beruf,

A⁷   Dm   A⁷   Dm
Rosenkes mit mandlen, schlof zhe yeedele, schlof,

                 A⁷   Em   Dm
Schlof, zhe yeedele, schlof zhe yeedele schlof.

English:
To my little one's cradle, comes a new little goat snowy white,
The goat will trot to market, while mother her watch will keep,
To bring you back raisins and almonds, sleep my little one, sleep,
My little one, sleep.

Layla, Layla (Hebrew Lullaby)

Alterman—Zaira

```
Em            Bm        Em
Layla, layla, haruach go veret,

               G      D⁷ G
Layla, layla, homa hatsa meret,

B⁷            Am        Em
Layla, layla, kochav mezamer,

B⁷    Em     B⁷     Am
Numi, numi, kabiet haner,

B⁷    Em     B⁷     Em
Numi, numi, kabiet hanar.

D⁷    B⁷ G B⁷     Em     B⁷     Em
Layla, layla, numi, numi kabiet haner.
```

Layla, layla, itsmi et eynayich, layla, layla, baderach eylayich,
Layla, layla, rachvu chamushim, numi, numi, shlosha parashim,
Numi, numi, shlosha parashim.
Layla, layla, numi, numi, shlosha parashim.

Layla, layla, echod haya teref, layla, layla, sheni met bacherev,
Layla, layla, vezeh shenotar, numi, numi, et schmech lo zachar,
Numi, numi, et schmech lo zachar.
Layla, layla, numi, numi, et schmech lo zachar.

Repeat 1st Verse

English:
Night, night, the wind is growing stronger, night, night, the treetops are rustling,
Night, night, a star is singing, sleep, sleep extinguish the candle,
Sleep, sleep, extinguish the candle.
Night, night, sleep, sleep, extinguish the candle.

Night, night, close your eyes, night, night, on their way to you,
Night, night, galloping in armor, sleep, sleep, are three riders,
Sleep, sleep, are three riders.
Night, night, sleep, sleep, are three riders.

Night, night, one fell prey to beasts, night, night, the other by the sword,
Night, night, and the one that was left, sleep, sleep, has forgotten your name,
Sleep, sleep, has forgotten your name.
Night, night, sleep, sleep, has forgotten your name.

Repeat 1st Verse

(S,C,SC)

Em ... B7 ... Em

La - la, lay-la, ha - ru -ach go ver - et, Lay - la,

G ... D7 ... G ... B7

lay - la, ho - ma hat - sa mer - et; Lay - la, lay - la ko -

Am ... Em ... B7 ... Em

chav me - za - mer, Nu - mi, nu - mi, ka -

B7 ... Am ... B7 ... Em ... B7

bi - et han - er, Nu - mi, nu - mi, ka - bi - et han -

Em ... D7 ... E ... B7 ... G

er. Lay - la, la - la,

B7 ... Em ... B7 ... Em

nu - mi, nu - mi ka - bi - et han - er.

125

Suliram

Indonesian
C. C. Carter

```
      C    F    G⁷        C    F       C
Suliram, suliram, ram, ram, suliram yang manis,

    F    G         C
Adu hai dung suhoorang,

        G⁷                      C
Bidjakla sana dipan dang manis. La

C            G⁷     C   G⁷ C
Tingi la, tingi si matahari, Suliram,

              F      C     G⁷ C
Anakla koorbaumati toortambat, Suliram,

      F       G         C
   sudala lama saiya muhnchari.

    G        G⁷         C
Barusuh klarung saiya muhndabat.
```
Repeat from the beginning.

English:
Early in the morning, as the sun was rising, I saw a water buffalo being killed in the field. O my darling, darling I've waited for you so long, at last I have you, I won't let you go. Hush, baby.

Pete Seeger learned this lullaby, adapted into a love song by a young Indonesian, Mas Daroesman.

(Pronounce *a* as in father; *i* as in *ee* in meet, *u* as in *oo* in room, and roll your *r's*.)

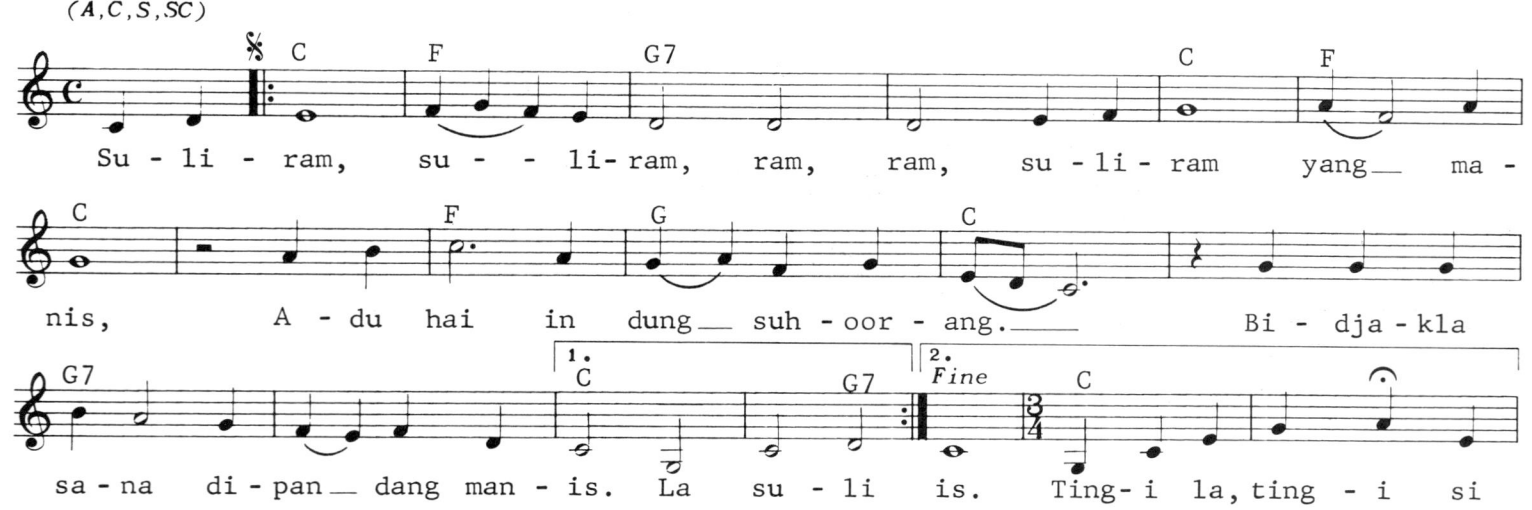

ma - ta - ha - ri, Su - li - ram, An - a - kla koor-bau-ma - ti toor-tam-

bat, Su - li - ram, su-da-la la-ma sai-ya muhn - cha - ri.

Ba - ru - suh kla-rung sai-ya muhn - da - bat. La Su - li-

Hajej Muj Andilku (Hush-a-bye My Angel)

Czechoslovakian Lullabye
Alma Turechek

C   F C
Hajej, můj andílku, hajej a spi,

          G⁷ C
Matička kolíbá děťátko svý,

Hajej, nynej, dadej, malej,

          G⁷ C
Hajej, můj andílku, hajej a   spi!

Hajej, má Hančičko, hajej tiše,
Panenka Maria tobě píše,
Až napíše cedulicku,
Tak ti ji položí na ručičku.

English:

Hush-a-bye, my angel, hush-a-bye,
Mother is rocking her little baby,
Hush-a-bye, go to sleep my little one,
Hush-a-bye, my angel, hush-a-bye and sleep.

Hush-a-bye, my little Hannah, hush-a-bye, softly,
The Virgin Mary is writing to you,
When she finishes the little note,
She will put it in your little hand.

Transliteration:

Hi-yay mui andilku, hi-yay a spee,
Matichka koliba dyetiatko svee,
Hi-yay, nin-ay, da-day, ma-lay,
Hi-yay mui andilkui, hi-yay a spee!

Hiyay ma Hanchichko, Hi-yay tizhe,
Panenka Maria tobeh pizhe,
Ashe napizhe sedulichku,
Tak tee yee polozhee na ruchichku.

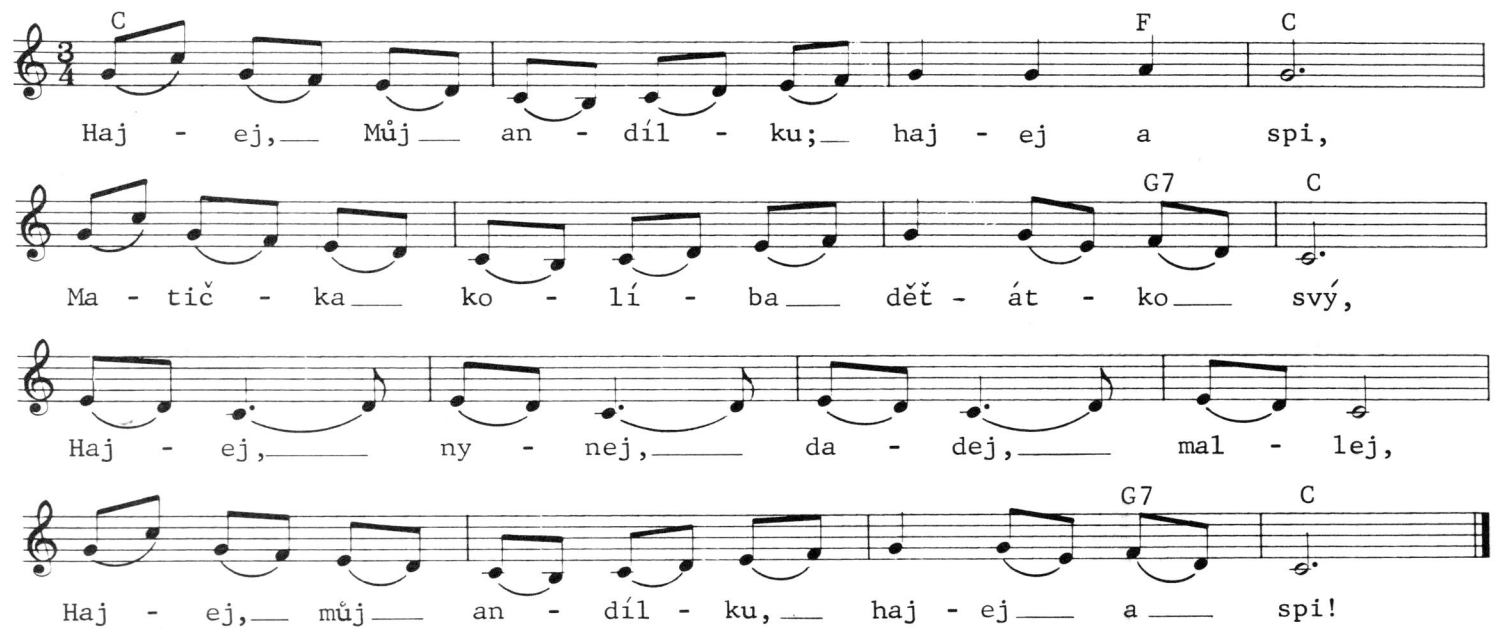

128